With Feet of Clay

May 2024

To Earl and Char

With deep gratitude for meaningful friendship in Christ

Bob Lindess

With Feet of Clay

Pastoral Confession—A Memoir

ROBERT J. LUIDENS

RESOURCE *Publications* · Eugene, Oregon

WITH FEET OF CLAY
Pastoral Confession—A Memoir

Copyright © 2024 Robert J. Luidens. All rights reserved. Except for brief quotations in critical publications or reviews, no part of this book may be reproduced in any manner without prior written permission from the publisher. Write: Permissions, Wipf and Stock Publishers, 199 W. 8th Ave., Suite 3, Eugene, OR 97401.

Resource Publications
An Imprint of Wipf and Stock Publishers
199 W. 8th Ave., Suite 3
Eugene, OR 97401

www.wipfandstock.coma

PAPERBACK ISBN: 979-8-3852-1972-8
HARDCOVER ISBN: 979-8-3852-1973-5
EBOOK ISBN: 979-8-3852-1974-2

VERSION NUMBER 040224

To my immediate family,
a boundless blessing, each and every one:

Ed and Ruth, my parents

Don and Carol, my siblings
Peg and Louise, their life partners

Mary, my wife
Emily, Karie, and David, our children
Matt, our son-in-law
and
Katherine and Isaac, our grandchildren

Contents

Preface | ix
Acknowledgments | xi
About the Author | xiii

1 Gift | 1
2 Night on Bear Mountain | 5
3 The Cost | 9
4 Really | 14
5 Biblical Profits | 18
6 Call | 23
7 Before and After | 29
8 Attentive | 34
9 Good and Faithful Daughter | 38
10 Like Father, Like Daughter | 41
11 Hope | 47
12 With Feet of Clay | 50
13 Omniscience | 57
14 Pressure | 61
15 Friends | 66
16 Only Silence | 69
17 Keepers | 72
18 Miriam's Shoes | 79
19 Bar-Jonah | 83
20 Table for All | 89
21 Broken | 93
22 Pillars and Salt | 99

23 Decisions, Decisions | 103
24 Issues | 107
25 Whisper | 111
26 Counterintuitive | 115
27 Let the Children | 119
28 Blackout | 122
29 Shepherding | 126
30 How Could I Not? | 130
31 Restored | 133
32 Service Station | 137
33 Privilege | 140
34 God Rest Ye | 145
35 Eulogy? | 150
36 Equity | 153
37 Enlightened | 158
38 Missed | 162
39 Voice of the Victim | 165
40 Neighbor | 169
41 Pastoring the Baton | 173
42 The Price Paid | 176
43 Our Kin Joseph | 180
44 Unspeakable | 186
45 Old Friends | 191

Preface

SIX MONTHS INTO MY retirement after thirty-five years in pastoral ministry with two wonderful congregations, the earlier urging of a dear parishioner once again grabbed hold of me. For several years prior to my retirement, Ellen had quietly but persistently urged me to make note of experiences and learnings from my ministry. The goal? A book that could then be shared with those who might find those reflections to be of interest, if not inspiration. Unable to ignore Ellen's counsel, I ultimately published what I presumed would be my one and only memoir. Entitled *The Kingdom Will Come Anyway—A Life in the Day of a Pastor*, it is primarily comprised of several dozen memories from my life experiences as pastor to those two congregations, one in central Kansas and the other in upstate New York.

That first memoir was published in early 2020, just a handful of days prior to the onset of the COVID-19 pandemic descending with crushing weight on the whole globe. Along with so many during the subsequent month after month of worldwide shutdown, I then inevitably found solace in reading countless books. One such stirring volume, recommended to me by a dear friend, was Jon Meacham's *The Hope of Glory—Reflections on the Last Words of Jesus from the Cross*. On a mid-winter day, I sat down in our rocking chair, Meacham's tome in hand. Three hours later, a welling up had begun deep within. And before I had even risen from that chair, I knew it. I was to continue writing. But this time I was to address any number of experiences I had avoided confronting in my first memoir.

Over the course of the next many months, I gave myself permission to relive—and now retell—some of those experiences. To my surprise, and even fascination, the following unfolded. Without originally planning to do so, more often than not, somewhere embedded in the draft of almost every one of those new chapters was the expression "I confess." Hence the subtitle of this, my second memoir.

Confession is a complicated word. It carries with it well more than one meaning. In this memoir, its use at times infers admission of my failures—all too many to count, sadly. But at other times its use points to my beliefs—sometimes in a religious sense, sometimes otherwise. Regardless of its varied uses, though, I sincerely trust confession to be very, very good for the soul. Such is unarguably the case for me. I sincerely hope it will be likewise as you read, as well.

* * *

Many are quick to remember that Joseph, the eleventh of Jacob's twelve sons, is described in the Old Testament as having a remarkable gift of dream-interpretation. Lesser known is the Old Testament character of Daniel. While celebrated for his prayerful survival in the den of lions, Daniel, like Joseph more than a millennium before him, also became a royally celebrated interpreter of dreams. In Daniel's case, as described in Daniel chapter 2, he shocked Babylonian monarch Nebuchadnezzar with a simple but startling parsing of that king's dream about a statue. Said statue, ostensibly of Nebuchadnezzar himself, had a head made of gold, but with less valuable—and less strong—metals below the neck. The statue's feet, Daniel pointed out, were made of iron, but mixed with clay. The latter inevitably imperiled the whole statue's survival. Having feet of clay betrayed that statue's vulnerable, even mortal, condition.

Derived from Daniel's commentary about that statue's feet, today many still make reference to a person's having "feet of clay." More often than not, that expression implies that person may appear to be strong, even unimpeachable—but is, in fact, as vulnerable to the common weaknesses of humanity as everyone else. I, for one, confess—there's that word—to having feet of clay. Many of the chapters in this memoir serve to prove that confession beyond a reasonable doubt.

My prayerful hope is each reader of the chapters comprising this memoir will find both humbling evidence of human shortcoming, as well as heartening witness to divine restoration. For, I confess, our loving God has fashioned each of us with feet of clay, and—not but—forever embraces all of us with arms of compassion.

Acknowledgments

As with my first effort at authoring a memoir, many individuals have blessed me with insightful counsel, exceptional editing, and steadying affirmation. Those listed below are but a few of the many.

Ellen Howie, whose urging a decade ago led to the composition of my first memoir, continues to represent many of my dear ones by embodying encouragement beyond measure.

Glenn and Nancy Wagner, steadfast pillars in so many ways, remain a faithful witness to the essence of patient friendship.

Peg Luidens, a heartening loved one as my dear brother's wife of more than half a century, spurred me on, chapter after chapter, with thoughtful encouragement throughout.

Jill Russell and Gordon Wiersma, my pastors in retirement, graciously offered solicited comment on various pieces I felt led on occasion to forward to them in draft form.

Peter Everts, clinical psychologist and brother in Christ, offered gentle but lasting counsel about various issues that found their way into my confessional ruminations.

And finally, my wife Mary continues to offer lasting support by patient reading of every word drafted for this memoir, as well as being my cherished companion each and every day.

* * *

As with my first memoir, the events embedded herein are recounted with a desire to capture the truthful essence of each instance described. However, with just a few exceptions all of the individuals have been given pseudonyms, and incidental details are frequently altered in order to protect confidentiality, as appropriate. I urge readers to derive benefit from the accounts without the necessity of identifying specific individuals or historical events described therein.

* * *

Verses quoted in this memoir are from the New Revised Standard Version Bible, copyright 1989, by the Division of Christian Education of the National Council of Churches of Christ in the U.S.A.

About the Author

THE AUTHOR WAS BORN in Iraq to missionary parents Edwin and Ruth Stegenga Luidens, who raised him and his older siblings Don and Carol in Iraq, Lebanon, and New Jersey. Bob attended Hope College in Holland, Michigan, where he met classmate and future wife Mary Koeppe. Mary received her medical degree from the University of Michigan, and Bob received his master's degree from Yale Divinity School. Thereafter he was ordained into the ministry of Word and Sacrament within the Reformed Church in America.

Bob and Mary served for three years as pastor and physician in the farming community of Lincoln, Kansas. They then moved to upstate New York, where Bob served for thirty-one years as pastor of the Altamont Reformed Church, while Mary pursued her advanced medical training as an Endocrinologist and then served on the faculty of Albany Medical College. They retired from those positions and moved to Holland, Michigan, where they now reside.

Bob and Mary raised three children. Emily is a mathematics instructor for a community college. Karie is a writer and artist. David is an orchestral percussionist, and is trained as a software coder. Bob and Mary continue to delight in their two grandchildren, Katherine and Isaac, children of Emily and her husband Matt Van Hook.

1

Gift

THE VISIT LASTED HALF an hour, if that. But those thirty minutes opened my eyes to a world thus far unrecognized, much less appreciated.

It was late spring, and I was nearing the end of the school year as a second grader. My family was coming to the close of living in a furloughing missionary house on the campus of our denomination's seminary in New Brunswick, New Jersey. In the coming weeks we would be moving again—the fourth time doing so in my young life. Our next destination? Beirut, Lebanon, well more than five thousand miles away.

In preparation for that major relocation, my mother had gently explained that I, along with my older siblings, would be allowed to take just a handful of personal toys and games. The costly shipping of all of our accumulated such items was out of the question. I would have not only to cull through all my treasures to select out the very few I would be permitted to take with me to our new home. I would also have to decide what would come of all that would stay behind.

That's where Petey came into play.

Petey was my best friend at school. We had met at the beginning of second grade, when he had begun to attend the public school I had attended since kindergarten. We sat near each other in class, enjoying moments of laughter during show and tell. We ate lunch together in the cafeteria, occasionally swapping items our mothers had seen fit to put in our lunch bags. But best of all we played side by side on the playground during recess, challenging each other to races and always ensuring we'd play on the same team when kickball games took shape.

Petey and I were inseparable—but only at school. When the school day ended, I walked home in one direction, and Petey in the opposite. We had never been to each other's homes, if for no reason other than our mothers never had the opportunity to meet. Petey had met Mom on a few occasions when she had volunteered as a classroom mother. But I had never met Petey's mother, since she had not been available to serve as a classroom volunteer herself.

Then came the day, towards the end of the school year, when Mom and I had the heart-to-heart talk about all my toys and games. Having explained as compassionately as possible how I would have to pick out the few things I could take to Beirut, she then said, "Now you can think about what you'd like to do with the things you can't take with you."

"It's up to me what to do with the stuff?" I asked Mom.

"That's right. It's your stuff, so you can decide where you'd like to give it." While I stared silently at her, trying to process this responsibility—no, this opportunity—she continued. "For example, you could take it down the street to our church and give it to them. They could put it in the nursery and playroom, and kids in the church could play with all of it there."

I well remember her making that reasonable suggestion. In retrospect, it's quite possible she had already spoken informally with the church staff about it, tentatively anticipating my concurrence with that simple solution. But before anything else was said, I recall responding, almost as if on cue, "No, thanks. I know what I want to do with my stuff."

Mom looked at me, curious. "What do you have in mind?" she asked.

"I think I wanna give it all to Petey."

Mom continued to look at me, still curious, if not a little surprised. "Petey? Petey Ramos?"

"Yup. He's my best friend, and I want him to have it all. He'll take care of it, and he'll have fun with it, even if I can't."

Though it's been more than six decades since our little exchange, I still clearly recall my mother tearing up and saying quietly, "That's a wonderful idea."

The following Saturday morning, Mom helped me load four boxes of my toys and games into the back seat of our '58 Chevy Biscayne. Off we drove, across town. I had no idea where Petey lived, but as we went I noticed we were leaving the western part of New Brunswick, heading to the eastern part, literally on the other side of the tracks on which the train took commuters into New York City. We left behind a neighborhood of single-family homes, and entered into a downtown community of tightly packed apartment houses and small businesses.

Mom found a parking spot on the street. Once she had her bearings, checking the address she had written down after an earlier phone exchange with Petey's mother, we walked up the outdoor stairs and found the right doorbell amongst many options. The name "Ramos" was hand printed next to the doorbell. When Mom nodded, I rang the bell. After a moment, I heard a quiet, female voice. "Quién es?"

"It's Bobby and his mother," responded Mom. "We're here."

To which Maria said, with a shy voice, "We'll be right there."

Ten seconds later I heard the thundering sound of Petey's feet charging down the stairs inside the entryway. The door flew open, and Petey shouted out, "You're here!"

Immediately behind Petey appeared his mother. Maria smiled at my mother, waved us in, and led us up to the third floor. Into their apartment we went, Petey grabbing me by my elbow, Maria gesturing to Mom to sit in one of the two chairs in the front room of their tiny two room apartment. To my surprise, Maria and Petey spoke rapidly to each other. In Spanish.

I had never yet heard Petey speak a word of Spanish during the entire school year. I confess it had never occurred to me to ask him if English was his first language. Nor had it ever occurred to him to ask the same of me. Though Spanish and Arabic had been our birth languages, our friendship knew no linguistic barriers. And as I was just beginning to understand, our friendship knew no ethnic barriers, either. Our friendship was rooted in companionship. Companionship not yet complicated by social boundaries or systemic fractures.

While Mom and Maria began to chat quietly, Petey pulled me into the apartment's one bedroom. He pointed to the small bed in the corner, proudly noting it to be his. The even smaller couch in the other corner was his mother's. When I asked where his father slept, he said, "In big cabins. On big farms far away from here. Where he helps pick things."

"Pick things?" I asked, confused.

"You know, things like apples. And cherezas." When I continued to look at him, uncomprehending, he said, "Like cherries." I nodded, still confused. "Papa is a trabajador migrante. He works on farms, going wherever farmers need things picked." I nodded again, tilting my head as an invitation for him to continue. "Papa works far away. Mama stays home with me and cleans houses in the city. We see Papa sometimes, but not for long." I recall having the vague sense his statement was both matter-of-fact explanation, as well as soulful cry.

Before anything else was said, Petey pointed to the end of his small bed, where a card table had been set up. Nothing lay on top of it. Petey declared, "That's where your stuff is gonna go!"

To which I said, enthusiasm instantaneously reignited, "It's all out in the car! Let's go get it!"

We rushed back into the front room, each imploring his own mother, one in Spanish and the other in English, to let us bring the haul up from the car. Down the four of us went, and then up we all came, loaded down with the four boxes. For ten or fifteen minutes, Petey and I pawed through Tinker toys, jigsaw puzzles, wiffle balls, and toy trucks. It was Christmas in May, both for Petey and me. The undiluted joy we each felt echoed the thrill he and I had had countless times on the recess playground and in our classroom. In retrospect, the unvarnished delight of the moment actually exceeded in many ways anything I had ever had to that point in my young life.

Then it was over. Mom and Maria gave each other friendly embraces. After Petey and I had jumped up and down with the indescribable joy only school kids can know, Mom and I left.

As we began to drive away, I recall looking over my shoulder, out the back window of the Biscayne. I remember spotting Petey in the front window of his little apartment on the third floor. He was waving. And smiling. As was I for a moment or two, until, I confess, I started to cry.

Mom, bless her compassionate heart, simply patted my left knee as she drove. No words were necessary. As transient as the time in the Ramos apartment may have been, it still was a moment of unadulterated humanity, of unparalleled blessing, of communion with one's priceless sibling.

A little later, once home, I headed upstairs to my bedroom, looking at the now emptied shelves that had earlier held all the departed toys and games. Did I miss them now? Not at all, I was surprised to admit to myself. But I knew in the depths of my little seven year old heart, I was going to miss Petey for the rest of my life. Profoundly.

All these years later, I still do. I've often wondered what came of the Ramos threesome. In this life I'll never know.

But thank God—truly, thank God—I can't wait to be reunited one day with Petey. With Pedro, God's priceless gift to me.

2

Night on Bear Mountain

It was a moment of pre-adolescent isolation. But also of unanticipated, soul-stirring awe.

I was twelve years old. Along with my family, I had moved from Beirut, Lebanon, to the foreign land of New Jersey some twelve months earlier. I was two weeks removed from having completed sixth grade. My loving parents, knowing I had not yet spent any time away from family thus far in my young life, decided it would be developmentally timely to ship me away to a sleepover camp. So on the first Sunday afternoon in July, off I bused for the hour long trip northward to the YMCA camp in the shadow of Bear Mountain, just north of the border between New Jersey and New York.

On arrival at the camp, I found I vaguely recognized a couple of classmates from the previous school year. But close friends? Not one amongst the hundred and fifty raucous boys enrolled for the thirteen day stay.

But that lack of friends was not the only discomfiting issue I had to deal with that first afternoon in camp.

So unfamiliar were both Mom and I about camp life in that kind of setting, the previous day she and I had packed a suitcase—not a backpack. Moreover, we had then prepped my new, winter-compatible sleeping bag by rolling it up only after first smoothly introducing into it both a long, white sheet *and* a multi-colored, wool blanket. On arriving at my cabin that Sunday afternoon, several of my new cabinmates stared in silence as I hauled in my suitcase and then unrolled the overstuffed sleeping bag. I proceeded quietly to unpack the suitcase and lay out my blanketed sleeping bag on a top bunk. Inevitably, my actions invited several looks of disbelief, a couple of rude jokes about "the skinny doofus" in their midst, as well as a host of rolling eyes of critique. To say I felt embarrassed doesn't do justice to the hollow feeling deep within my pre-teen soul.

That's how the thirteen days of woodland purgatory got its start.

Within, oh, one hour of my arrival, I was feeling the universally familiar ache of homesickness. It was paralyzing. Try as I might, I couldn't shake the yearning for my parents to come and rescue me—to take me away from this place of emotional isolation.

Over the next few days, the experience deteriorated even more. On Monday everyone was given a swimming test in order to determine what depth into the camp's Hessian Lake we would be allowed to venture. Having thus far never had any swimming lessons—not unusual for missionary kids in the Middle East—I was restricted to the three foot deep, roped-off section of the swimming area. While virtually all of my new cabinmates were allowed to swim daily out in the ten foot deep section of the lake, I stayed beachside with two or three others who glumly stared at the fun unfolding beyond the floating rope dividing shallow from deep.

Then there were the daily obligations to do what our cabin counselor called "manly stuff" in the camp's woodworking shop. Well, I knew what a saw was, and could even differentiate between flat head and Phillips screwdrivers. But had I ever made significant use of any of those tools? Nope. And guess what? Yup, virtually all of my new cabin compatriots were veterans of all things woodshop-related. By the fourth or fifth morning, I was daily relegated to being the "broom guy"—the ignoramus who was expected to sweep up everyone else's wood shavings on the floor, and not much more than that.

Ugh.

Each night I found myself counting down the number of days until my parents would pick me up and free me from my juvenile jailhouse.

The problem was, though, each of those nights, sweating profusely in my winter sleeping bag, I was aware that Night Eleven was drawing closer. Our cabin counselor had explained that on that night of the thirteen in camp, our whole cabin crew would hike three miles, up to the top of nearby Bear Mountain. There on its apex we would all climb into our sleeping bags and slumber under the stars.

The thought of spending a dozen hours outside, without protective roof or nearby bathroom, sent me into a despondency even more pronounced than I had thus far known since disembarking the bus that first Sunday afternoon. It is not exaggeration to confess I was in quiet terror that something unforeseen would inevitably descend upon me during the approaching night on Bald—uh, Bear—Mountain.

Finally, inexorably, day eleven arrived. Thankfully, our counselor informed all of us cabin charges our sleep under the stars that night would be just that. Under only stars, with no rain, or even clouds, in the forecast.

After supper in the dining hall, the dozen of us from the cabin set out on our hike through the woods and up the mountainside. I walked in silence, trying valiantly not to disclose my growing anxiety. Finally, we reached the peak of the 1,300 foot mountain. To my surprise, the mountaintop was a large, flat slab of rock, with no trees and only the expansive sky above. For an hour, as sunset approached, our counselor invited us to lay our sleeping bags out on the rock and then gather in a circle to share stories from our early childhood years. I sat in silence and listened as several of my more vocal cabinmates regaled us with comic instances of years past. To my quiet surprise, I found myself listening and chuckling, warming up to the moment.

Before we knew it, the sun had set and the sky grew dark. An unfamiliar, peaceful quiet descended on all of us. The counselor instructed us to climb into our sleeping bags and get some shuteye. "Tomorrow's your last full day in camp, guys," he noted. "Sleep well."

Into my sleeping bag I went. But while typically I would role onto my belly in order to fall asleep, not this time. Not in this setting. Instead, I allowed myself to lie on my back, looking up at the dark sky. And at the myriad collection of stars.

That's when it happened. Lying there in silence began as a moment of pre-adolescent isolation. But it became one of unanticipated, soul-stirring awe.

Absent any ambient light from nearby towns, the sky was both black and bright. The stars—including those in the Milky Way—shone in spine tingling clarity. I could barely believe my eyes.

For the first time in the better part of two weeks, I truly relaxed. I felt a kind of peace unlike anything I had yet known in my short life.

Some two months earlier, while paging through a recent *National Geographic* magazine, I had learned about a light-year—the distance that light travels in one Earth year. That distance is approximately six trillion—6,000,000,000,000—miles. Astronomers now estimate that the spherical diameter of the observable universe is more than forty billion light years. That is to say, a beam of light would take more than forty billion years to travel from one edge of the known universe to the other.

Lying on my back on the top of Bear Mountain, I stared at the stars that were visible to me. And it hit me: I was looking at stars that looked to be—and were—very distant from our own solar system. And yet, in the deep black spaces between those stars lay countless millions of other unseen stars, even galaxies, at incomprehensible distances into the universe. And all of it, seen and unseen to my limited vision, comprised God's creation. Where God was doing God's thing, making and shaping and renewing and loving.

It hit me. Or more to the point, it stirred me: "I'm lying here, a microscopically tiny presence in God's unimaginably immense universe, and yet God knows me. In the same moment God is caring for life forms on planets trillions and trillions of miles away from me, God is watching me. Is watching *over* me."

In that setting, in that moment, following a handful of days of some of the most lonely, isolating experiences of my pre-adolescent years, it happened. I realized I wasn't alone. I was in God's care. I was loved by the one who had fashioned me, who had given me a loving family, and who would never let me go. Would never let me be alone, no matter what.

There on Bear Mountain, looking up at the stars, in quiet isolation, I discovered awe. There on Bear Mountain, in what to that moment had been a time of draining desolation, I found myself embraced.

There on Bear Mountain, beyond any predictability, my fledgling faith was seeded.

For that, I am eternally—yes, eternally—grateful. To my parents. And to our God.

3

The Cost

"This begins to explain it all," I quietly mumbled to myself.

Planted quietly in a comfortable armchair, I put the book down and stared through the window. Just outside my dormitory the wind was howling, a mid-winter snow descending on the campus in west Michigan. A junior in college, I was working my way through my religion professor's latest assigned reading. The focus? German theologian Dietrich Bonhoeffer's *The Cost of Discipleship*. Coursing throughout Bonhoeffer's tome I was being introduced to his startlingly honest thesis that when one feels compelled to follow Jesus—to be a Christian disciple—one had better be prepared for any number of sacrifices. The costs, so to speak, of entering into the life of commitment to Christ are no small matter.

Bonhoeffer knew of what he was writing. A pastor and teacher living in pre-war Nazi Germany, he became an outspoken proponent of the way of Christ, rather than the way of Hitler. In 1937 he published *Nachfolge* ("the act of following"), reflections on Jesus's Sermon on the Mount. In due course the book's title morphed into *The Cost of Discipleship*. Now, less than four decades after its publication, Bonhoeffer's writing was striking a chord with me: "This begins to explain it all."

Growing up the youngest of three children of missionary parents, I had experienced any number of moments when the cogency of Bonhoeffer's thesis was on full display. Though I had minimal to no appreciation of that fact while living through those moments in the past, that was now beginning to change in my twentieth year. Staring out my dorm room window, three such instances were coming to mind.

Interestingly the first instance was one of which I had no personal recollection. But I had heard it described multiple times in such gripping detail by my mother that it was as if I could recall it as intensely as she. The year was 1955. I was not yet two years old. My family was living in Amarah, Iraq, where Dad and Mom were serving a mission station as, among any number of roles, evangelist pastor and teacher/women's and girls' group leader, respectively. Their eldest offspring—my brother Don—was seven. Up until that point in his young life, he had received his schooling in our foreign mission home, under the caring tutelage of our mother. But missionary kids at that time and place were expected, come Don's young age, to be shipped off to a boarding school in southern India, where they could receive an education far more akin to that of children growing up in North America or Europe.

Regrettably, that boarding school in India was some twenty-five hundred miles away from Amarah—a distance comparable to that between New York City and Phoenix. The one-way trip took several days. It included car, air, train, and bus transport. And those six boys and seven girls making that trek? Their ages varied from seven to seventeen, with the latter adolescents in charge. That's right. In charge of a twenty-five hundred mile journey through four countries.

It was that group of missionary children with which my seven-year-old brother traveled for the first time, without a parent or sibling accompanying him. My mother, years later, described for me what it was like for her to take her eldest child to the airport in Basrah, Iraq, where Don—clearly unable to appreciate in the least what he was embarking on—reportedly gave Mom a quick hug, hustled his way across the tarmac with heavy bags in hand, and climbed aboard the TWA Constellation. Understandably oblivious to the essence of the moment, he did so without turning around for a final wave to his family.

The pain experienced in that moment by our mother, matching that of countless other missionaries before and after her, was beyond description. Yes, the deeply rooted expectations that defined the typical missionary life in those times and locations were essentially non-negotiable. Mom understood that implicitly. And in understanding it implicitly, she had reason not to feel personally culpable for shipping her seven year old son off to a boarding school light years away. But in no way would—or could—that have lessened the soul-wrenching pain, and even guilt, of that moment in her young parenting life. To the contrary, she must have felt mortified. And in fact I know that to have been the case. She confessed it to me years later, during my high school years.

Now in college, as I sat looking out my dorm window, the cost of Mom's discipleship back in 1955 shocked me. Beyond words. How could it not?

And then, still gazing at the snowfall, a second instance of the costly dynamic of discipleship drifted its way into my mind. Now the year was 1963. Our family was stationed in Beirut, Lebanon—where, not coincidentally, my brother, sister, and I were all able to walk to school from our apartment building. That privilege had been unarguably a factor in our parents' decision to live and work there for three years.

But those three years were not easy ones for Dad and Mom. While my brother, sister, and I were all able to walk to our school, our father was constantly on the road. Actually, in the air. He was engaged in the development of a radio evangelism ministry, with the principal broadcast station located in Addis Ababa, Ethiopia. With exhausting frequency he would fly to Ethiopia. Then to Egypt, Turkey, Cyprus, and in between even to Switzerland and Germany. It was in the midst of Dad's resulting, countless home arrivals at Beirut's international airport, Mom would occasionally invite me to accompany her when she took a taxi to the airport in order to welcome him off another plane. Prior to the plane's touchdown, I loved racing up the terminal's stairwell that exited out onto the observation deck, then watching planes take off and land. When Dad's flight finally touched down on the runway, Mom and I would head back into the terminal and walk excitedly to the Customs exit door, through which Dad would then walk and welcome hugs from his wife and son. Those moments of welcoming my father home were always dear to me. At supper all five of us would trade stories of what we'd experienced in the days, if not weeks, since we'd last been together as a family.

But then there was that one airport reunion that was, in a heart-wrenching way, unlike all the rest. That one time that captured, albeit in a small way, some of Bonhoeffer's truism about the cost of being a disciple.

Dad had just flown in from Cairo, where he had been for the better part of a week. As he gave warm hugs to Mom, and then to me, he looked me in the eye and asked, "How are *you*, Bob?"

I recall saying something akin to "I guess okay, Dad." But then, without thinking about the implications or impact of my doing so, I queried, "When are you going away again?" I was simply curious.

Six decades later I can still remember, with stark clarity, the look that then defined my beloved father's face. His smile faded. A look of sadness, even despondency, replaced the joy of just a moment earlier. He dropped to his knee, took my shoulders in his hands, and looked me in the eye. I honestly don't recall exactly what he said. But I remember how he said it. It was with both solemnity and affection. And the essence was: "I'm home now. Where I want to be. With you, and Mom, and Don, and Carol." Though I don't recall tears, I've no doubt they were there, ready to flow from his loving eyes.

Years later Dad and I chatted about that moment. He described how my question, as innocent a question as a ten year old could ask, tore at his soul. It made unarguably clear to him the price of his Christian service was immeasurable. His son's simple question had peeled back the truth about the price of his father's vocational responsibilities. I had not asked, "How long are you staying home?" I had asked, "When are you going away again?" Some might say there's no difference between those two questions. The look on Dad's face proved otherwise.

Less than a decade later, I sat in my college dorm room, still looking out at the snowfall. Bonhoeffer's thesis about the costliness of following Jesus had brought those memories from both Iraq and Lebanon to mind. But then it elicited one final recollection—one unlike the first two, but deeply connected to them nonetheless.

It was the early spring of 1970. I was a junior in high school. Our family now resided in the foreign land—at least to me—of New Jersey. Six years earlier Dad had accepted an invitation to work in New York City as our denomination's executive director of all foreign missions. The new position meant a move from Lebanon back to the United States, which beneficially allowed us closer proximity to our relatives. The transition especially well suited Mom, enabling her finally to reconnect with her beloved parents. And once I acclimated during junior and senior high school to the vagaries of America's diverse culture, it suited me, as well. Dad's extensive travels continued, but his absences seemed to be somewhat more tolerable to Mom. She had begun to build new friendships with New Jersey neighbors, and ultimately became the director of Christian education in a nearby congregation. She was a perfect fit, and she thrived in her new responsibilities.

Then the third incident unfolded. Had Bonhoeffer been present, I suspect he would have quietly nodded his understanding.

It was mid-week. Dad's carpool van had brought him home from New York City thirty minutes earlier. Mom, he, and I were now seated around our dinner table. We were enjoying the meat loaf and mashed potatoes she had prepared for our supper. Per usual, after detailing for the two of them my school day activities, I then chewed away and listened quietly to my parents' gentle exchange about their days, as well. It was in that context that the shocking unfolded.

Having described one staff meeting or another Dad had endured that morning, he then said, "And guess what? I got a call at noon from Mort in Geneva, Switzerland."

"Mort?" my mother asked, betraying a look of confusion. Or maybe it was suspicion.

"Mort Gauthier. With the World Council of Churches. He's the one who helps place clergy in international, English-speaking churches." Mom nodded silently, apparently sensing what was coming. "Mort told me my name came to mind with respect to the little congregation in Kabul, Afghanistan. Their current pastor will be retiring this summer, and he thought—"

"No."

I stopped chewing. Maybe even stopped breathing. I stared at Mom, who had just spoken her one word assessment of the proposal Dad had barely begun to describe. Then I swiveled my tense neck in Dad's direction and stared at him. While Mom was already putting another forkful of meatloaf into her mouth, Dad's mouth was, one could say, agape. For maybe five seconds, a truly deafening silence reigned supreme. Then Dad said, "Okay."

That was it. No more mention was made at that table of Mort, or of Kabul, or of any kind of move away from New Jersey. The discussion—discussion?—was over.

Given the simple fact I had never, ever witnessed my parents engage in an overt argument, I realized I was on uncharted territory. Later that evening, lying in bed and failing miserably to go to sleep, I said to myself, "I guess that was an argument?" And then, feeling no small measure of pride in my mother, I also mused, "I think she won."

All such adolescent comedy aside, I've thought about that moment at the dinner table on countless occasions. One such occasion was while sitting in my dorm room, just four years later, staring out at the snowfall. Bonhoeffer's commentary on the cost of being a disciple of Christ was now the context. And just as I had pondered Mom's watching Don board the Constellation almost two decades earlier, and just as I had recalled Dad's falling to his knee in the Beirut airport about a decade earlier, I now added to the list my parents' "argument" four years earlier. While all three instances were unique, they nonetheless were knit together, it seemed to me. They were knit together by the nature of the cost that each reflected. The cost of discipleship.

Sitting in my dorm room, I wondered to myself, "What costs lie ahead for me?" Did I know the answer to that unsettling question? Not in the least.

But over the half century since then, I confess that on any number of occasions I've found myself admitting, "Oh, Dietrich, were you ever right."

4

Really

"Are you really a Christian, Bob?" he asked.

I was so caught off guard by the question, for a moment I stood there on the sidewalk, mute. I then managed to respond, albeit still puzzled. "Yes, Liam. I am."

"Huh," he said. "Under the circumstances, I've begun to wonder."

Just what were those circumstances? The answer to that question is an old story, in two senses of the expression. My exchange with Liam was old in that it unfolded almost a half century ago. But it was also old in that it's the kind of exchange that's been around for all too long, and continues even today.

Liam and I were seniors on the same Christian liberal arts campus in Michigan, just two months shy of our graduation. We had known each other all four academic years, although not particularly as best friends. We had been enrolled in the same courses at least twice, had played pick-up basketball on several weekends, and both regularly had attended the college's thrice weekly morning chapel services. Moreover, most every Sunday morning we each participated in the campus's sizeable worship service, led by the college's esteemed chaplain. Liam would sit in the pews, while I assisted the chaplain up front as student lay liturgist each week, leading the several hundred students assembled in the large chapel in the opening prayers and readings.

Why now Liam's short but loaded question about my "really (being) a Christian?"

It was precipitated by a two day visit on campus of a man in his early thirties. Luke Smith had been invited by the college chaplain to share his unfolding life story as a pastor who happened to be gay.

The Rev. Smith was a resident of a major city on the east coast, serving on the pastoral staff of that city's Metropolitan Community Church. That congregation, along with many others nationwide with a comparable name, identified as home to gay Christian men and women who felt unwelcome—or were barred from membership—in most mainline churches. Luke's ministry with that congregation was increasingly heralded for his gentle but strong advocacy for the place and role of what decades later is known as the LGBTQ+ community, including within the wider Christian church around the globe.

It should be noted that, while the struggles members of the LGBTQ+ community face today remain intense and exacting, in contrast fifty years ago those struggles were monolithic. Luke could well attest to those struggles, his own and of those to whom he ministered.

It was those challenges from the mid-1970s upon which Luke was invited to reflect as the two day guest of our college chaplain. He was welcomed as worship leader during the morning chapel service, as well as presenter in a couple of class settings.

I had the privilege of sitting in the pew as Luke preached, and was deeply moved by his thoughtful, honest reflections. But that early morning uplift very soon dissipated. Now sitting in the back of a packed lecture hall for successive afternoon classes with Luke as guest speaker, I very soon found myself surprised, then stunned, and finally enraged. In both class settings, Luke became the object of caustic comments, demeaning questions, and outright verbal assault from many students. Classmate after classmate responded to Luke's presentations with statements essentially questioning how with any integrity he could possibly self-identify as a Christian at the same time as being honestly open about being gay. To his credit, Luke maintained calmness in his responses, refusing to take the grossly evident bait to engage in vitriolic reactivity. No matter how assaultive many of the students in the lecture halls brazenly opted to be, Luke displayed a steadiness of spirit and conviction unlike anything I imagined anyone could under such unsettling circumstances.

The following day, after Luke's departure for the airport to fly home, I stewed. I confess to feeling institutionally embarrassed, as well as personally appalled. After trying to process in intense conversation with the college chaplain what had transpired during Luke's visit, I decided I could not ignore the moment. I could not remain silent regarding my spiritual disappointment in so many of my fellow undergraduates—men and women who self-identified as Christians, but who had just attacked and demeaned a fellow Christian who happened to be gay.

So that evening I sat at my desk and worked at drafting a letter to the editor of the campus's weekly newspaper. After several hours of writing and rewriting I took the typed piece in hand, walked across the darkened campus, and delivered it to the newspaper's student editor. I had arrived at 11:55 p.m., five minutes before the deadline for that week's forthcoming edition.

The following, somewhat disjointed piece is what this twenty-one year old, white, cisgender male composed for the college community:

> *This past week many of us on campus had the unusual opportunity to meet with Mr. Luke Smith, a genuinely honest Christian homosexual. The impact of his visit prompts me to share with fellow Christians a concern raised by discussions centering on the issue of the Christian homosexual.*
>
> *I have become deeply troubled by the Christian church's occasional lack of acceptance of persons struggling with burdensome problems which it has historically shunned and condemned.*
>
> *In the case of homosexuality (which I do not here wish to Biblically condemn nor support), we Christians have come to turn our institutional backs on those who are struggling with the realities of homosexuality in our society. As a result, among these men and women are devout Christians who feel only ostracism and rejection by fellow Christians.*
>
> *I fully feel the difficulty which the institutional church has had in relating to the "gay" Christian. Yet Christ demands that our love not be a discriminatory love. That love should be ready to express itself in earnest confrontation.*
>
> *Confrontation should be with open hearts, honestly aware of the realities of all personally human struggles, be they of the homosexual, the mentally ill, the forgotten aged, or the imprisoned criminal.*
>
> *We each must realize the worth of life of every man and woman, for God's love and forgiveness can be accepted by all.*
>
> *We as Christians are not called to judge, but to serve. I suggest in that light that we each examine our readiness to love those whom we have socially rejected. Similarly, may we as a Christian community more readily serve those whom we have neglected as a result of their lives in our society.*

Two days later that week's newspaper appeared campuswide. Leaving the dining hall after supper, I picked up a copy and found the letter on page six. Above the seven short paragraphs was the following title: "Luidens lauds 'gay' Christian." I vividly recall smirking when I read those four words. "Did the editor even read my letter?" I wondered aloud. Clearly the editor did, but then opted to frame the letter in a manner that had little if anything to do with my intended message.

Folded newspaper under my arm, I began walking back to my dorm. As I did, I heard Liam calling to me. Here he came, accompanied by two of his buddies, and with his own copy of the newspaper in his right hand. "Bob, can I ask you a question?"

"Hi, Liam. Sure. What's up?" I asked.

"Are you really a Christian, Bob?"

I was so caught off guard by the question, for a moment I stood there on the sidewalk, mute. I then managed to respond, albeit still puzzled. "Yes, Liam. I am."

"Huh," he said. "Under the circumstances, I've begun to wonder." He then stretched out his right arm, pointing the folded newspaper at my chest. "I've just read about your love of gay people, and I can't help but wonder if your so-called Christian faith is nothing but fake."

I wish I could report the ensuing conversation on that sidewalk proved constructive and restorative. But I'm unable to do so. To the contrary, our exchange was brittle. Liam was as assaultive, quite frankly, as had been so many in the two classroom settings just two days earlier. Along with his well-intentioned buddies, Liam made it crystal clear that they could see through the veneer of my so-called Christian faith. That they knew my heart, and it wasn't in a good place. That they were now undoubtedly convinced I was in Satan's grasp, and was a disgrace to the Christian world.

Within a handful of minutes Liam and Co. strolled away from me, nodding with certainty to one another the truth had been spoken: I had been put on notice that any standing I might have had to that point in time within the wider Christian student body on campus was now history.

Did I survive the moment? Of course. But not without realizing I had stepped somewhat naively into the cauldron of the wider Christian church's brokenness. Was the pain I felt anything at all comparable to that of Luke and so many others in the wider world of the church and beyond? Not even close. But that pain is one I've chosen not to forget. It's an injury I've recognized as essential to remember, because it speaks in admittedly minor ways of the grievously severe suffering of so, so many others—all at the hands of those who call ourselves Christian, and who readily, even insistently, refuse to call others likewise.

Until and unless we in the institutional church acknowledge this soul-wrenching reality, we will fail again and again to reflect, much less reveal, the very one from whom we draw the name of Christian.

5

Biblical Profits

"Well, this sure isn't Dad's old Bible book stall anymore," I whispered to myself.

The year was 1975. I was barely four months removed from my college graduation. Just two nights earlier I had arrived by jet from New York, beginning nine months of work as a volunteer. My commitment was to serve the ecumenical mission in the small island nation of Bahrain in the Persian Gulf. Sponsored by my church denomination back in the U.S., I was assigned to provide assistance to the sizeable book store that sat prominently on a main avenue in Bahrain's capital city, Manama. In close proximity to the book store were also a hospital, church, and school—all dynamic results of many decades of Christian missionaries' service to the residents of Bahrain.

In truth, I discovered quite quickly I knew all too little about the book store prior to my arrival that week. I had been told it was the modern-day version of what had originally started as an eight foot by eight foot book stall in the busy *souk*, or marketplace, in the older, inner city part of Manama. That book stall had been, in fact, a product of my own evangelist father's efforts to engage Bahraini Muslims in conversation about the Christian faith. My parents had served as full-time missionaries in Bahrain for several years back in the late 1940s. During that time Dad felt led, on a once weekly basis, to take a small box of Arabic language Bibles and then sit quietly in the stall, offering them free of charge to curious Bahrainis. Oftentimes he would then chat with them in Arabic about Allah—God—from their contrasting faith perspectives. Prior to my flying off to Bahrain in the fall of 1975, Dad had told me about those dynamic 1940s conversations in the book stall, speaking warmly of the friendships he had enjoyed with many gracious Arabs.

Though I knew that stall had disappeared, now replaced elsewhere in the city by a much larger, more modern book store, I still carried the image of my father's having sat in that original book stall a quarter of a century earlier, sharing in quiet conversation with his Bahraini neighbors about their complementary, but contrasting, faiths.

Then reality hit me in my volunteer's face. A day after my arrival in Bahrain, Konrad, the Danish manager of the book store, gave me a quick tour of the modernized facility. Looking a lot like the Barnes & Noble in my home town back in New Jersey, it had three levels. By rough, conservative estimate, ninety-five percent of its books were in English. The Arabic language book section was off to the side, indicative (I would learn in due course) of the very limited number of Bahrainis who opted to browse the store's shelves. Rather than anything vaguely reflective of the book stall in the nearby *souk* of the 1940s, this book store now clearly catered to the English-speaking market—a market that apparently clamored for racy romance novels and French cuisine cookbooks.

At the close of the rather brusque tour of the book store proffered me by Konrad, he led me into a back room where the weekly shipment of boxes from the UK arrived with the store's new books. He explained my job as a volunteer would include correlating the boxes' contents with the bills of lading, ensuring the British book distributors were not overcharging us. In his distinctive Danish accent, Konrad then instructed me to "stock the books in their appropriate sections—fiction, travel, non-fiction, history, culinary, and even religion." The last word was spoken with a subtle smirk and a shrug of shoulders. It was jarring beyond measure to my still jet-lagged soul.

Attempting to engage in some form of dialogue with my new boss, I responded, "Quite a variety of books you have here."

"Well of course," Konrad responded. "We have to sell all kinds of books in order to survive. How else could we pay our bills?"

Betraying the naiveté of a twenty-two year old, I then said, "I presume the book store gets a good bit of financial support from any number of church denominations in the U.S. and elsewhere, including my own denomination."

To which Konrad responded, with another smirk and shrug, "Oh please. Your own denomination has stopped giving *any* financial support to this book store. Didn't you know this?"

"No," I responded. "I had no idea."

Konrad then described how, in the previous several years, my denomination back in the U.S. had formally adopted a policy that many ventures initiated by their own missionaries—including the book store, church, hospital, and school in Bahrain—were to move into the Western world's model of becoming self-supporting. No longer would the previously named "mission book store," therefore, receive any significant financial support from the churches in the U.S. If it were to survive, much less thrive, it would have to generate capital adequate to cover all of its own expenses.

Konrad concluded his explanation in a matter-of-fact manner, stating, "That's why the book store's management team here in the Persian Gulf hired me away from my large book business back in Copenhagen: to help the book store here make enough money that it won't have to close."

With that, he headed into his office, leaving me to my boxes of books and my now troubled thoughts. "This store is now meant to be entirely self-supporting? And it was my own denomination that decided this? Well, this sure isn't Dad's old Bible book stall anymore," I whispered to myself. And it wasn't in spirited humor that those words washed quietly into the stale air of that work room. It was in dispirited gloom—even perplexed irritation.

Over the subsequent weeks and months the real life implications of what Konrad had disclosed to me became increasingly evident. Wherever and whenever profits could be generated by the sale of the store's product, they were made. Or more truthfully, they were maximized. In fact, I soon became both witness and party to said marketing practices in, of all places, the transit lounge of the nearby international airport that served Bahrain.

A few months after my arrival, Konrad approached me with a "request." He needed me to staff a small but highly profitable business location run by the book store. A few years earlier, I learned to my surprise, the book store had won sole proprietorship of the tiny but busy book store in the Bahrain airport's transit lounge. Because Bahrain sits essentially midway between Europe to the west and Asia/Australia to the east, it was a principal stopover for carriers flying between those distant continents. As a result, large 747s operated by British Airways, Air France, Qantas, and others, would disgorge their several hundred, in-transit passengers for an hour of stretching while their planes would refuel. Those passengers would inevitably wander over to the wee little book store in one corner of the transit lounge, checking out the hundreds of paperbacks and several dozen varieties of post cards (displaying picturesque Bahraini sites) the book store's staff had put on display. Purchases would then be made. And in that process, profits were generated in mind-boggling manner. In due course I ended up sitting behind that book store's counter, mission volunteer of all things, and participated in a capital windfall machine. By way of example . . .

Konrad insisted on charging approximately fifty cents for each postcard that originally cost the book store around ten cents. But that four hundred percent markup wasn't the full story. The travelers, oftentimes carrying only English pounds or Japanese yen, were expected to pay for the postcard in Bahraini dinars. That inevitably prompted a foreign currency exchange surcharge, which provided the book store the opportunity to make even more profit on the purchase. A proffered twenty pound note would be converted into dinars, but with a ten percent currency exchange surcharge. If the travelers then didn't want their change in dinars, but rather in yen, an additional ten percent currency exchange surcharge would be incurred. By the time a postcard—originally costing the book store ten cents—had been purchased with a twenty pound note, the profit margin was staggering: the book store had captured upwards of four to five dollars in profit. And yours truly, mission volunteer in the footsteps of my evangelist father decades earlier, was party to a money-making operation precipitated by my own *Christian* denomination's insistence the mission book store become self-supporting.

Suffice it to say, week after week of engaging in the above marketing scheme soon elicited from me not just immobilizing embarrassment but gut-wrenching guilt. I confess, in fact, that by the end of my nine months of volunteer service in that emotional and spiritual morass, I departed Bahrain questioning what the "mission" of the book store really was—and what my denomination back in the U.S. really thought it was accomplishing by its decision to mandate the book store become fiscally self-supporting.

Over the next several decades of ministry within that same denomination, I occasionally found myself confronted with circumstances reminding me of the Bahraini book store and its mandate to be self-supporting—a mandate that ultimately had given birth to unseemly profiteering. On any number of occasions, serious-minded Christians, including me, found ourselves in the middle of well intentioned deliberations about assets and budgets. And whether in full view, or buried just below those conversations' surface, was the issue of how to ensure the institution's financial security going forward. Almost inevitably discussion would evolve into how to maximize adequate inflow of money in order to guarantee long-term survival. In truth, most of those deliberative discussions were constructive and honorable. But occasionally they were less so. On rare but memorable occasions during such meetings, comments and asides would be made suggesting an opportunity was presenting itself for the congregation or local judicatory to "raise a few extra dollars"—dollars that could be "invested for the future." But the investments in question were not in people or programs, but in CDs or securities. And those investments' yields weren't referred to as profits, but as aids to the institution's long-term viability.

The above would bring to mind, even if in only faint echoes, the Bahraini book store's 1975 mandate—*mission*, even—of becoming self-supporting.

Do I blame the institutional church, be it local congregations or sizeable denominations, for being fiscally attentive to long-term, financial viability? No. To ignore such concerns would be irresponsible, and even unfaithful. But that does not allow for the church to move subtly—and at times unabashedly—in the direction of giving greater emphasis to self-serving financial security than to self-sacrificing faithful service.

For it was Jesus himself, seeing fit to speak again and again about the temptations of monetary idolatry, who asked, "For what will it profit [you] to gain the whole world and forfeit [your] life?" (Mark 8:36)

6

Call

THERE I WAS, SITTING—AND stewing, in all honesty—in the back pew. And of all times, that's when it happened. I felt a call. Into the ministry.

Was I expecting it then and there? Not in the least. In fact, because I was in a bit of a sour mood, a call into the ministry was, oh, the last thing I could have ever predicted experiencing at that moment in time.

Even close to five decades later, it's still something akin to a mystery to me. Yet that was when I sensed—one could even say heard—God's undeniable insistence I was now to begin the process of preparing to become a pastor.

And it's all that led up to that moment in the back pew that still makes it all the more mystery-filled for me . . .

Some twelve months earlier I was in the fall semester of my senior year in college, trying, in all good faith, to discern God's will for me upon graduating the next spring. To that end I had had several intense conversations with various individuals I regarded as trustworthy mentors. They included loved ones, esteemed professors, respected classmates, and the college chaplain, whom I served as student assistant. The upshot of those exchanges? I decided to apply for admission to both seminary and graduate school. The latter was in the area of Arabic studies—an academic field that intrigued me, given my relative fluency in Arabic as a young child born to missionaries living in Iraq. Regrettably, I had lost most use of that amazing tongue when my family had moved from Iraq to the U.S. before my fourth birthday. Now as a twenty-one year old I sensed that introduction to Arabic at the graduate level might reinvigorate my latent language skills, thereby enabling me to enter into a career that would make constructive use of bilingual capabilities.

So Thanksgiving weekend of my senior year I chose to remain on campus. Cooped up alone in my dorm room for the four day weekend, I churned out several lengthy applications to seminaries and universities. That Monday I recall walking to the nearby post office, and away those thick packages went, accompanied by a quiet prayer on my lips.

Come late winter I heard back from those esteemed institutions. Admission was offered to seminary. But most intriguing to me? One of the graduate programs—that of the University of Michigan—did as well. The latter, in fact, shocked me by offering an incentive of full tuition, plus a yearly stipend to cover basic expenses, all to the end of my working towards a PhD in Arabic linguistics, culture, and literature.

Upon receiving those notices of admission, I realized I yet remained uncertain which path to pursue. One day I would find myself drawn to pursue theological training; then the next day I admitted to a significant curiosity—even pull—to do Arabic studies. By early spring I realized my ambivalence was impossible to ignore. So I decided to inquire of both the seminary and the graduate school whether they would be willing to hold my admission for a year. To my surprise and delight, they both agreed to do so. And their doing so opened up for me a third pathway—one that might give me opportunity for more definitive discernment of God's will for me than I was feeling at the time.

That third pathway, postponing immediate entry into either seminary or graduate school, was to accept an invitation from my church denomination's office of Adult Voluntary Services (AVS). I had communicated extensively with that office's staff two years earlier. During my sophomore year, it was looking more and more likely I would be drafted by the Selective Service System to provide alternative service as a conscientious objector. My draft board had graciously given me allowance to fulfill my two years of alternative service by working with missionaries in the Middle East. President Nixon, however, ordered the cessation of the military draft just prior to the date I would have been ordered into that alternative service. His doing so allowed me to complete my full four years of undergraduate studies uninterrupted.

Now, in the spring of my senior year of college, my earlier consideration to serve for two years in the Middle East came back into play. I decided to pursue, for one year's duration, my previously offered volunteer service to my denomination's mission station in the island nation of Bahrain. The AVS office's staff and I agreed that I would fly to Bahrain in early September, following my springtime college graduation. I would take a full year's leave from my academic studies, during which time I could assess more carefully whether, on returning to the U.S. thereafter, I should head to seminary or to graduate school.

But that summer between my college graduation and my flying off to Bahrain for the year of vocational discernment, things got delightfully more complicated. I began to date my future wife.

Mary and I both graduated together earlier that spring. Prior to graduating, we had come to know one another; our roommates had become engaged and seen fit to introduce Mary and me to each other. Mary, I learned, was heading off to medical school that fall—in Ann Arbor, of all places. Ann Arbor, where I had been offered a position in the PhD program in Arabic studies. Moreover, we discovered we each had summer work opportunities on our college's campus. During that summer after our graduation, prior to her starting medical school and my heading oversees for a year of volunteer work in the Persian Gulf, we dated. And we fell very much in love. By the end of that summer, we were in serious conversation about marriage, albeit how and when to actually have a wedding being totally unclear to the two of us.

Summer's end saw Mary moving to Ann Arbor, and me flying to Bahrain, some seven thousand miles away. The day prior to our heading off to our two distinct destinations, we could well attest to dear Juliet's assertion that parting indeed is such sweet sorrow.

That September while Mary began the monolithic venture of training to become a medical doctor, I began my work as a mission volunteer in the Middle East. In my back pocket, so to speak, were the documents from both seminary and graduate school, each promising me admission to their respective programs the following fall when I would be back in the U.S. As you might guess, the admission from the Arabic studies graduate program became my daily enticement. Knowing Mary would be in Ann Arbor for the next four years, I knew all I had to do, in order to be in proximity to her, was to accept the PhD program's offer. Barely settling into my new life in Bahrain, I began to envision myself foregoing seminary in favor of Mary—uh, graduate school.

Then early in October, a full month into my volunteer work in Bahrain, the unexpected began to unfold. Missing both Mary and my family back in the U.S., I received a letter from my father. Writing from our family home in New Jersey, he informed me he had arranged a major work-related trip to include a twenty-four hour stopover in Bahrain. He would be flying in early November from Geneva, Switzerland, on his way to Manila, Philippines, and had booked his flights so that he would have a twenty-four hour stopover in Bahrain. His arrival would be at midnight on the first Saturday in November, departing at midnight Sunday. I was overjoyed at the prospect of Dad's impending visit, figuring we would make full use of those two dozen hours for lengthy walks and talks as a twosome.

Then I blew it.

Excited at the prospect of Dad's arrival in a few weeks, I informed Hal, the missionary pastor of the interdenominational church I was beginning to attend and enjoy. I was aware Hal and Dad knew each other; Dad in fact had been one of Hal's predecessors in that same mission church a quarter of a century earlier. But when I told Hal of Dad's coming stopover, he immediately said, "Well, then I'll definitely have to ask him to preach for me for our Sunday evening service!"

I remember reacting to Hal with a look of surprise, if not irritation. "But Hal, Dad's stopping over for that one day in order to see me, not to be your guest preacher." I confess the idea of sharing Dad with anyone else, much less the whole congregation as guest preacher, irked me. "I'd prefer him sitting with me in the pew rather than being up in the pulpit, Hal."

But Hal was not to be deterred. "Oh, I know your Dad. He'll do this for me. He's done it before on previous stopovers here in Bahrain." And before I could find words to object any further, Hal continued, "When you write to him today, tell him I'll welcome his filling pulpit for that Sunday evening's service. He'll say yes, I'm sure."

And you guessed it: Hal's wish would become my dear father's command.

On the first weekend of November, I met Dad at midnight as he disembarked the jumbo jet from Geneva. We drove from the airport to my small apartment in the mission compound, grabbed a few hours of sleep, and then spent Sunday morning and afternoon chatting about all things Bahrain and vocation. The time with him was wonderful, but all too short. Then late afternoon arrived, and Dad switched gears. From focusing on all that he and I had begun to think out loud about up to then, he did what Hal's invitation necessitated: he pulled from his briefcase notes for his guest sermon for that evening's service. Rather than being able to continue our time in constrained but nonetheless enormously significant conversation together, we sat in silence in my apartment, Dad preparing to preach, and I feeling ignored. All because of Hal. And because of what two clergymen, including my own father, allowed somehow to detract from a precious, fleeting father/son moment in time.

Seven p.m. arrived. Some one hundred worshippers gathered in the mission church's sanctuary. Dad and I had parted ways some thirty minutes earlier in order for him to meet with Hal as they finalized details for the service. I wandered into the sanctuary, opting to forego my relatively new seat towards the front. On this occasion, feeling sorry for myself, and no small measure of frustration—well, ire—towards Hal, I flopped into the back pew, as far from the pulpit as I could get.

I confess even today, almost five decades later, I thought about getting up and wandering out of the sanctuary. The only thing keeping me in my seat was the simple fact I was curious to hear what Dad would share from the pulpit.

The service began. I tried to sing the hymns, but did so only sullenly. I made the effort to listen thoughtfully to the readings, but barely to any real benefit. Finally, when introduced by Hal, my father walked to the pulpit. He prayed for God's blessing. Then he began to preach.

In the back pew I sat, still stewing a bit about the unfairness of it all. "He should be sitting back here with me, not standing up there," I silently muttered to myself. "*I* need him more than all these others sitting here do."

And that's when it happened. Of all times, that's when it happened. Almost half a century later, I still recall it as if it were just yesterday. Or even just now. I felt a call.

While staring at Dad way up front, saying Lord knows what, I heard a voice within me. Deep within me: "This is what you are to do, Bob."

I sat there, barely hearing my earthly father's voice coming from way up in the front of the sanctuary. Instead, I heard a stronger voice. An insistent voice. A gracious voice. "This is what you are to do. You are to be a pastor."

I remember sitting absolutely still. And I remember the irksome feelings of just a moment earlier inexplicably vanishing. Where I had been feeling self-pity, something entirely different was now rushing in. A sense of clarity and of purpose now insisted its way into my thoughts. Into my heart. I don't know how else to describe it.

"I am to be a pastor, Lord?" I asked silently, already knowing the answer.

There I sat for the balance of the service, awash in as unexpected a sense of purpose as I could have ever thought possible. "I'm to be a pastor," I then said silently, but not only to myself. And then: "I'm meant to go to seminary next year." This simple acknowledgment came with a wondrous peace—peace that confounded me immediately. "I'm not meant to go to graduate school. I'm not meant to move to Ann Arbor . . ." I confess to tears beginning to wash over my eyes as soon as that realization, and its implications, hit home.

When the service ended, I sat alone in the back pew. Hal escorted Dad to the entryway of the sanctuary, where I watched my father greet dozens of departing worshippers. It was moving beyond measure to do so. It hit me I was beholding not just Dad, but a prefiguring, if you will, of my vocational future. My vocational call.

In the next two hours Dad and I drove back to the airport. His midnight departure for Manila fast approached. But during those two hours our conversation was unparalleled. It was unprecedented, for obvious reasons. Where earlier in that same day I had droned on and on about my vocational ambiguity, now I shared with him what had transpired while sitting in the back pew, listening—not primarily to him, but to a different voice. A more commanding voice. One who was calling me.

Bless him, Dad simply let me talk for those last minutes before checking in for his flight. His embrace, rather than his words, spoke of his understanding. And of his love.

In short order I wrote to Mary in Ann Arbor. I described to her all of the above. And, not surprisingly, she supported me in my inevitable decision to forego graduate work in Ann Arbor, heading instead, following my year of service in Bahrain, to seminary in Connecticut.

Do I understand all of the above? Heavens, no. But do I question it? Not in the least. Because when one hears a call from within—from deep within—it cannot be ignored.

7

Before and After

ON INSTANCES ALMOST TOO many to count since retiring I have found myself revisiting that totally unanticipated—yet eerily predictive—conversation with my dear mother.

I was twenty-three, she fifty-five. I was a first semester seminary student in Connecticut. She was a Christian education director in a local parish in New Jersey, but increasingly compromised by the cancer that had been diagnosed more than two years earlier. My father was traveling overseas, leaving Mom home alone—a condition not all that unfamiliar to her, given Dad's current responsibilities working with Christian leaders throughout East Asia and the Pacific.

I had arrived by train and bus earlier in the evening, enjoying a quiet supper with Mom. Exhausted from the day's activities, she accepted my offer to do the dishes. She headed upstairs, readied herself for bed, and invited me to come visit with her bedside once I had finished cleaning up in the kitchen. Half an hour later I climbed the stairs and saw she was already in bed, sitting up and reading. I stuck my head through her bedroom door, and welcomed her smile and gesture to come in. I pulled up a chair and sat in close proximity to her.

That's when the unexpected unfolded.

Mom reached out to take my hands in hers. That in its own right was not unfamiliar. But the look on her face was. She smiled, but only mildly. Gazing intently into my eyes, she said, "I've been wanting to talk to you." I nodded. "It's about your choosing to go to seminary." I nodded again. She looked away for a moment, then back at me. Her look almost pierced my heart. "Are you sure you're supposed to be going into the ministry?" she asked quietly, almost urgently.

A word about my mother. She was the granddaughter and daughter of pastors, having grown up in parsonages from infancy straight through her college years. She had then fallen in love with the son of a pastor. That young man, soon to be her fiancé, headed off to seminary while she finished her last two years in college. In the years thereafter, she and her new husband entered into ministries that took them to Iraq, Bahrain, Lebanon, and ultimately New Jersey, where she and I now found ourselves talking bedside. Her question about whether I indeed felt I was "supposed to be going into the ministry" was undoubtedly influenced by five and a half decades of her immersion in the ups and downs, the joys and sorrows that define the vocation of ordained pastoral ministry.

So, though her question struck me as being out of the blue, in truth it was anything but. It was a deeply compassionate inquiry. A fittingly parental query that any daughter or son should rightly honor by answering honestly.

"Am I sure I'm supposed to be going into the ministry?" I squeezed her hand gently but firmly, saying, "Yes, Mom. I believe I have a call to serve in the ministry, wherever God sees fit to send me." We looked each other in the eye, and then I asked the question begging to be posed. "Why do you ask?"

I honestly had not the faintest idea how she would answer—in no small measure because I had no inkling she would ask me that question in the first place. But, true to her caring ways, she responded, "I'm concerned about you." I nodded again, while she remained silent for a bit. Then she explained. "I'm concerned that you may not be able to get work in churches in the next few years. There are more young pastors out there than congregations looking to call a new pastor." I nodded, though I found myself mildly surprised to learn about an overabundance of clergy relative to open parishes. "I just don't want to see you go all the way through seminary and then not be able to get work." She looked away for a moment, silent. It was an awkward silence, though. Sensing she was not quite finished with her thoughts, I waited. "I don't want you to get hurt. By the church." I waited. "By not being able to get a job, I mean."

It was in that moment I began to question whether I was hearing the whole story. Or even the real story.

With mild trepidation, I ventured a response. "I appreciate your concern for me, Mom. I really do. I'll be honest and say I wasn't aware it may be hard for me to get a call to a parish ministry. In fact, I confess I've been presuming that won't be an issue for me." She squeezed my hand, nodding. And tearing up. "What is it, Mom?"

I waited, until she said, "I don't want you to get hurt. That's all."

"Thank you. I'm sure you don't."

With that she said, "Tell me about school. Your classes, professors, and all. I want to hear about them." The smile continued. But her eyes betrayed a kind of uncertainty. Maybe even anxiety.

Twenty-four hours later, I sat on the New York to New Haven commuter train, staring out the window, revisiting our bedside chat. I kept replaying that brief exchange in which my dear mother had said two things, but maybe meaning only one. She had expressed her concern I may face challenges in securing a call to a parish. But she had also said, seemingly in that context—but maybe only vaguely so—she was afraid I might be hurt. By the church.

Looking out at the darkness of the Long Island Sound, it hit me. Mom may not so much have been worried about the overabundance of young pastors competing for a limited number of ministry openings. Rather, Mom may have been far more worried—fearful, in fact—I was walking vocationally into a work place far more hurtful than many might know.

But *she* would know. She, in fact, had reason to know.

As the train hummed along, I allowed myself to see her son through her eyes. I allowed myself to see myself in the context of the years and years of hurt she had witnessed as the granddaughter, daughter, daughter-in-law, and wife of pastors. I allowed myself to feel some of her angst—even dread—that her offspring was walking into the ecclesiastical turmoil that had exacted so much from her forebears, as well as from her own husband.

What mother, what father, would not feel trepidation, if not terror, that their offspring was walking into a vocational setting defined by potential trauma.

Mom truly did not want me to be hurt in—or by—the church.

* * *

Some three decades later I sat in the study of a dear friend. Dave was a clinical psychologist, as well as ordained clergyperson. I had just spent more than an hour detailing for him what had prompted my wife to urge me to seek out a therapist.

For the previous year or more I had begun to experience disruptive symptoms that were impeding my ability to function in healthy ways within my pastoral ministry. I had been serving my second parish for well more than two decades. But as a consequence of unforeseen stressors in my ministry—both within my own parish and within a sister parish nearby, to whom I was given supervisory responsibilities while they searched for a new pastor—I had increasing difficulty sleeping soundly, staying focused in my day-to-day ministerial tasks, and maintaining a needed sense of emotional stability.

Now in Dave's study, I spelled out in explicit detail all of the above. He listened carefully, asking occasional questions for clarification. When I finally ceased talking, he said, in a quieting way, "You know, don't you, Bob, what your diagnosis is."

"Dave," I responded, "I have no idea."

"You have PTSD." I stared at him, both in disbelief and shock. He clarified, saying, "You have post-traumatic stress disorder."

Not so much intending to be comical, as simply being confused, I said, "Dave, I was born in Iraq, but I've never served there."

He smiled a bit, and then said—said, not asked—"Where do you work?"

The focus of his statement—not question—was understood by both of us. I worked within the church.

From that instant on, Dave gave me the permission I had not known how to give myself up to that point in my ministry. Or actually, in my life. He gave me permission to identify and acknowledge the many and varied ways pastoral ministry is the context for stress that can—no, will—impact any and every soul who has ever entered into the vocation. He compassionately, but sternly, urged me to identify each and every stressor which had come with that vocation. That process felt uncharted. But it was essential. If and when I were to begin to regain a sense of well-being, both personally as well as professionally, it would require an unblinking honesty. It would demand of me an unflinching openness to the hurt I had experienced in the church.

It wasn't more than a few weeks into this psychologically and spiritually therapeutic process, through which Dave sat with me for countless hours in his study, that I began to recall sitting bedside with Mom so many, many years earlier. What she had conveyed, albeit in a convoluted way, was a concern that was now proving legitimate. Her son, so many years after her passing, was having to come face to face with his mother's fear.

In the years since Dave and I began the reparative work of naming my PTSD, and forging a pathway into healing—and ultimately into retirement—I've hearkened back to my mother. And by extension I've hearkened back to her grandfather, father, father-in-law, and husband. I've inevitably wondered how much one or more of them might be in a position to sit alongside me in Dave's study and say, "Oh, that explains it. That explains me."

Maybe more significantly, in the years since my restorative work with Dave, I've pondered about my current peers in pastoral ministry. About those who, called by our gracious and healing God, serve within potentially corrosive settings, slowly paying the price without the benefit of a friend, a peer, a professional calling them to honest self-awareness. Inviting them to a place of soul transparency when and where healing can begin.

How I would today deeply value another quiet, bedside conversation with my acutely attentive, astonishingly prescient mother. I suspect, in all good faith, she and I will have quite a few things to discuss once, by God's grace, we meet again.

8

Attentive

No matter how hard I tried, I could not for the life of me get either one of them to pay attention to me. And it wasn't for lack of trying.

Roland, Julie, and I were sitting on a stage of sorts in front of some two dozen other seminary students, as well as our esteemed professor, Dr. Green. His class was entitled An Introduction to Pastoral Care and Counseling. It was a yearlong course for students preparing for various professional ministries, including in the traditional parish setting. Dr. Green, a clinical psychologist, used a teaching model that included Monday and Wednesday lectures, leading up to Friday role playing sessions. Following the two days of lectures about that week's focal topic, the Friday setting would include two or more of us students somewhat bravely volunteering to be part of an unscripted, acting scene in which that week's topic might apply to real life circumstances.

The week in question—when Roland, Julie, and I raised our hands—was designed by Dr. Green to underscore the challenging demands of attentiveness. For two days he enumerated countless signals—both verbal and non-verbal—a pastor should watch for when interacting with parishioners. By the end of that week's second lecture, I had several pages full of notes, as did all of my classmates. Given Dr. Green's masterful teaching skills, I anticipated the Friday session would give undeniable evidence of his students' capacity to be incomparably attentive.

Was I ever proven wrong.

Friday morning arrived. Dr. Green did as he did every week, indicating a need for three volunteers for the role playing. A number of us put our hands up. Roland, Julie, and I were selected. On Dr. Green's instruction the three of us headed to the front of the classroom, where he had positioned three chairs, two side by side, with the third facing the two. He instructed Roland to sit in the one chair, and Julie and me to sit in the two chairs that were side by side. He then explained to all in the classroom that the setting was a pastor's study. Roland would play the part of the pastor, while Julie and I would serve as a young couple who were here for pre-marriage conversation. A year earlier, Dr. Green explained, "Pastor" Roland had agreed to officiate at "our" wedding, now just three months away. The conversation we were to act out was ostensibly intended to finalize details about the service, including the music. Dr. Green noted that "bride-to-be" Julie was a graduate student in a music conservatory, while "groom-to-be" Bob was a new employee in a marketing agency.

After those introductory comments, Dr. Green did what he would always do before the Friday role playing would begin. He handed to each of the three of us our own, small file card, upon which he had handwritten instructions. On his cue, we each read our own file card silently to ourselves, giving no indication to anyone else what was written on our card. I read the following on my card. "*You, the groom, have begun to develop major misgivings about moving ahead with the marriage. You haven't expressed those misgivings to anyone yet. During this session, use whatever body language necessary to convey your misgivings, both to the pastor and to your fiancée. But do NOT state those misgivings verbally, unless specifically invited to do so.*"

While I read my instructions to myself, "Pastor" Roland and "bride-to-be" Julie read theirs in silence, as well. Along with all of our classmates sitting in the audience, none of the three of us knew what instructions the other two had been given by Dr. Green. After a silent half-minute of reading by the three of us, Dr. Green instructed us to begin.

"Pastor" Roland began by saying, "Julie and Bob, it's great to see you again!" His enthusiasm was unbounded.

Immediately Julie responded. "Pastor, I'm so excited to be here! I couldn't wait to discuss the wedding music with you, because there's so much I want to have happen: the prelude, the processional, a solo that my roommate at the conservatory might sing, the recessional! Everything!" Julie was practically bouncing in her chair with eager anticipation of the wedding planning about to unfold in the pastor's study.

As if on cue, Roland sat forward in his chair, turning definitively in Julie's direction, leaving me clearly off to the side. Remembering my instructions, I then began my silent messaging of misgivings about the impending nuptials. I sighed quietly. When neither of the other two seemed to notice, I sighed again, but this time with gusto. Still no recognition of my non-verbal message. So, I then twisted my torso not so subtly, turning my full body away from my "fiancée" Julie. I folded my arms, mimicking a two-year-old's signal of displeasure. I did not smile. But I said not a word.

Meanwhile, Roland and Julie dived into the music. Back and forth they went, with an unmitigated enthusiasm that would have had me guffawing had I not been so intent on adhering to my role. While the excitable twosome jabbered on about Pachelbel's "Canon in D" versus Beethoven's "Ode to Joy," I fidgeted. I crossed my legs with a flourish, and then re-crossed them in the other direction. I rolled my eyes. I puffed out my cheeks with a theatricality that would have embarrassed most thirteen-year-olds. But I still said not a word.

Meanwhile Roland and Julie pressed on with their planning, utterly oblivious to me. No matter how hard I tried, I could not for the life of me get either one of them to pay any attention to me. And it wasn't for lack of trying.

In the midst of this comedic venture, I stole a glance out at the students who were watching the scene unfold in front of them. Some had their mouths agape. Others were unabashedly shaking their heads in disbelief. A few were holding their hands in front of their mouths, safeguarding against raucous laughter.

Meanwhile, Roland and Julie agreed, with undiluted joy, that Beethoven was a must.

At that point, I seriously—yes, seriously—contemplated standing up and walking out of "Pastor" Roland's study. But before I managed to do so, Dr. Green intoned quietly, "Thank you. That should just about do it."

From the onlookers out in the class room came a palpable shudder of relief, if not an expulsion of pent-up exasperation.

Dr. Green walked up to join the three of us. As he did each Friday, he took a chair and sat down beside us. As was customary at this moment in time, he then invited each of us to read what was on our cards.

"Pastor" Roland read first. "*You have had several sessions with the groom and bride, and are now ready to plan the music for their impending wedding. Styling yourself a music buff, you are eager to discuss the options with the bride-to-be, a musician of some renown in your congregation. Her enthusiasm is energizing for you.*"

"Bride-to-be" Julie then read. "*You are excited about your impending marriage, but especially about the wedding, during which your musical gifts will be on display for everyone in attendance. The pastor and you need to agree about the music, so the pastor can convince the organist what to play.*"

Finally, Dr. Green instructed me to read my card. When I had finished doing so, Roland—a good friend of mine—stared in disbelief at me. So did Julie.

The class as a whole, to their credit, withstood the temptation to react aloud, in no small measure because most of us had already had comparable, jarring moments "on stage" in previous weeks' role-playing experiences.

It should take no great imagination to picture how the balance of the class session unfolded. Dr. Green didn't have to point things out. Instead, the entire assembly of us students found ourselves commenting at length about the grossly evident inattentiveness on display during the role playing. Roland and Julie, to their undying credit, spoke at length about how each realized, after the fact, how entirely inattentive to me they had been during the role playing. They both commented on how engrossed they had been with their own agenda, thereby entirely losing any awareness of my proximity, much less of my comedic, silent body language. Neither had *any* recollection of the non-verbal signals I was attempting to convey during their enthusiastic dialogue about music.

Notably, to a woman and man in the class room, not one intimated that they would have done anything other than what Roland and Julie had done. Such was the powerful didactic prowess of Dr. Green. From week to week each and every one of his students found it more and more necessary—more and more beneficial—to look ourselves in the mirror and take note of so, so much we needed to learn prior to entering into caring, compassionate—yes, attentive—ministries.

Not surprisingly, that session, when I was instructed to play the reticent groom-to-be, came to mind countless times over the decades since. Again and again—be it while planning a wedding or sitting in a committee meeting; be it while talking with a parishioner in my study or leading a junior high youth group discussion—I have had to remind myself to listen. To watch. To be attentive.

Have I been successful in doing so? Sometimes. But on too many occasions, I confess, no.

Which is why it behooves me, over and over, to recommit to Dr. Green's sage counsel. It behooves me—as it behooves everyone—to listen, to watch, with the kind of attentiveness our ever-patient God has to each and *every one* in God's beloved family.

9

Good and Faithful Daughter

My heart ached, given what she looked and sounded like. But I confess my heart also raged, given what had been done to her. By her friends, no less.

My beloved mother sat in a living room chair, a blanket wrapped around her bathrobe in order to fend off the early November chill seeping its way through the nearby window. I sat across from her, having arrived for a short weekend visit less than an hour earlier. A second year seminary student, I had decided to drive from Connecticut to New Jersey in order to spend a quiet day with her.

As hard as it was to witness, it was increasingly clear Mom was drawing close to the end of her life. Diagnosed with renal cancer several years earlier, she had endured surgery and chemotherapy. But those treatments were proving ineffective. She was now essentially limited to her bedroom, sleeping a good portion of each day.

On my arrival she had insisted on coming downstairs to visit in the living room. Now, with each of us planted in our chairs, she had begun to fill me in. She had described her most recent phone consultation with her oncologist, as well as a warm visit from the pastor of the congregation whom she had been serving for several years as a director of Christian education. Those exchanges, with doctor and minister, had evidently been uplifting.

But then Mom's face transformed. Her look went from peaceful to tortured. The change was almost surreal. But it was undeniable. "What is it, Mom?" I asked. For a moment my mother remained silent. Then she began to tear up, although her expression was not so much one of sorrow as of pain. Almost one of fear. "Mom?" I asked again.

She then responded with trembling voice, "Evelyn came to see me this morning. And she brought two of her friends from church." I nodded, recalling Evelyn was one of Mom's many friends from our home congregation in town. When I was about to respond with a platitude-filled note of thanks for good friends, I stopped. Mom's expression seemed to repel any such comment. Instead, she choked out the following. "I apparently don't have enough faith." She wrung her hands. Tears erupted. "My faith isn't what it should be."

At this, I recall sitting forward in my chair, ready to walk the two steps over to her chair. But something kept me from that gesture, at least for the moment. Instead I said, "I don't understand, Mom. What do you mean your faith isn't what it should be?"

Mom looked down at the floor, not at me. "Evelyn and her friends: they told me if I only had enough faith I would be getting better, rather than worse." I resisted interrupting her, though I confess I was tempted to do so. She continued. "They prayed with me, asking God to give me the faith I need to get better. And while they prayed, they laid their hands on me, saying they were asking God to renew my heart so I would be able to be healed." Again I resisted the urge to interrupt. "Now," she continued, "I feel like I'm a failure as a Christian. I don't have enough faith."

Looking at my dear mother through my own tears, my heart ached, given what she looked and sounded like. But I confess my heart also raged, given what she had just described to me—what her friends, no less, had done to her. Sensing she had said all she was able to say, I finally rose from my chair, walked over to her, and knelt in front of her. I then took her shoulders in my hands, looked her in the eye, and said, "Mom, you are a woman of unfathomable faith. What Evelyn and her friends said to you was wrong. It was hurtful." She stared at me. She did not nod her agreement, but gazed at me with what I can only describe as hunger for good news. "They may have meant well by coming to see you and saying what they said, but they couldn't be more wrong. You're not sick because of too little faith. You're sick because of the cancer."

She looked at me with an evident yearning to believe what I had just said. "You don't think my lack of faith is causing me to get sicker?"

Resisting the temptation to bellow out "Of course not," I tempered my voice. "No, Mom. I do not think any lack of faith is causing you to get sicker." Then, trying desperately not to let the righteous anger I was feeling towards Evelyn and her partners define my conversation with Mom, I said, "Your faith is deep. It is known and honored by God. The last thing God wants you to feel is your faith is inadequate."

Then, causing me to tremble in sadness, she whispered, "I don't feel like my faith is deep. I feel like a shell of myself." Then she wept. We held each other, warmly, wordlessly.

In due course, we again began to talk. But in some ways our conversation was secondary to our embrace. Decades later, in recalling that moment, it doesn't surprise me what our mother/son hug communicated. It disclosed far more the mysterious truth about God's healing presence to the sick than would have been any verbal effort to contest the threesome's injurious words about the sick one's faith.

More than four decades since that living room moment, what I find undeniable is how it was a precursor to many comparable moments that would unfold during my years of pastoral ministry. Again and again I would find myself in quiet but excruciating reflection with the dying, who would disclose to me a confusion, if not a terror, about faith. Oh so frequently I sat bedside with a person facing end of life pain and isolation. That person would beg to be assured their faith—or the lack thereof—was not the cause of their suffering. In many if not most of those moments, I hearkened back to my mother and me sharing in a wordless hug, rather than a wordy explanation. In many if not most of those moments I offered God's quiet embrace, which spoke volumes more than words might have.

What Evelyn and her friends did to—not for, but to—my beloved mother was presumably rooted in well intended scriptural interpretation (see Mark 5:34, for example). But their actions, I'm convinced, were wrong. They left the vulnerable one devastated rather than uplifted. They caused pain upon pain, even if unintentionally.

As self-evidently wrong as behavior such as that of Evelyn and her friends was, it never ceases to amaze me how common it remains within the sphere of the community of faith. For whatever reasons, the church has enabled the persistence of the corrosive presumption of "If only." *If only your faith were strong enough . . . If only you trusted God . . . If only you believed rightly . . .*

No. Our loving maker does not abandon the sick, no matter the condition of their faith. Our healing redeemer walks alongside the sick, regardless of the condition of their spirit. Our gracious God does not add to the turmoil of the dying. Our compassionate God embraces.

My beloved mother breathed her last less than two months later. She did so while her adoring husband, daughter, sons, and daughters-in-law surrounded her with affection. And she did so while her immeasurably loving God gently held her, whispering to her soul, "Well done, good and faithful daughter." (see Matthew 25:21)

10

Like Father, Like Daughter

It was early in the morning of December 27, 1977. Lying awake, I glanced teary eyed at the bedside clock. It read four a.m. Though the house was now quiet, I nonetheless knew I wasn't the only one who had yet to fall asleep, given all that had unfolded in the last few hours and days—and years, for that matter. Only fifty-six years old, my beloved mother had passed away earlier that evening. Now, just hours later I was already searching for words to explain some of the mystery-filled circumstances surrounding her death.

Her battle with metastatic renal cancer had lasted well more than three years. During that fraught stretch of time, she had been forced to endure surgery, chemotherapy, and various other medical measures, none of which proved effective in warding off cancer's corrosive assault on her body. The final weeks of her life had seen her increasingly bedridden. Though in retrospect it had become unarguably evident Mom's death was fast approaching, conversation to that effect within our immediate family circle—Dad, my beloved siblings, and our life partners—had been fairly limited. The irony, it hit me lying in bed just a handful of hours after Mom had quietly died, was that *she* had been more aware of—and driven by—her death's imminency than the rest of us.

On Christmas evening, essentially twenty-four hours before Mom's passing, our little family had sat around her bed, sharing in quiet Christmas gift exchange. Mom was semi-propped up on two pillows, lying under a heap of blankets, drifting in and out of sleep. But at one point during our unwrapping of various presents, she spoke up. "Ed," she said to Dad, "give them the gifts." She did so with a stridency that was almost jarring. As weak as she had become, she now directed our father to do as she said, no questions asked. Dad did as she implored. He located several packages and proceeded to hand them out to my sister, to my brother and his wife, and to my wife and me. When we opened them, we discovered items from the Middle East—ones Mom had evidently identified as being essential gifts for our three little family units. When all three gifts had been examined, we conveyed our thanks to Mom. She promptly sank back onto her pillows and drifted off to sleep. In retrospect, from her end-of-life perspective she had just accomplished a final act of familial care and generosity.

The next day unfolded quietly. Mom remained in bed, in and out of sleep. That evening, all six of us once again gathered in her bedroom in order to share in another quiet celebration. It was my sister Carol's twenty-eighth birthday. Mom had indicated an unflinching insistence we share in birthday cake and gift-giving in her bedroom, rather than elsewhere in the house. After supper we shared in a reprise of the Christmas evening's gathering around her bed. "Happy Birthday" was sung to Carol, and a few gifts were handed to her, including one more from Mom and Dad.

And then it happened. With our now having completed both the Christmas gift exchange of the evening before, and then the birthday presents as well, Mom died. Dad noticed Mom was now lying absolutely still under the covers. She had stopped breathing. A frenetic reaction unfolded, including the calling of an ambulance, the professional efforts of two paramedics trying to revive Mom, and the subsequent race of the ambulance to the nearby hospital. All to no avail. Because Dad's dear wife—our amazing mother—had already well moved on. In fact, I confess feeling an unarguably intense sensation while the paramedics had begun cardiopulmonary resuscitation on the floor next to her bed. While they worked valiantly to revive her, I still today, nearly half a century later, recall a yearning to say to them, "Stop. She's gone. She's no longer here."

Some handful of hours later, I lay in bed, staring at the nearby clock. It read four a.m. But given all that had unfolded during those previous two evenings, not to mention the months and years preceding, I wasn't ready for sleep. Instead, as I presume happens to most everyone in any comparable circumstances, I pondered. I wondered. And I began to remember.

Many recollections from my childhood, adolescence, and young adulthood, flooded into view. I revisited countless instances when my mother had displayed grace, joy, and life. I recalled innumerable circumstances when she had embodied strength, determination, and conviction. I was overwhelmed. With sadness, yes. But also—maybe especially—with gratitude.

Then, in the midst of that misty-eyed, early morning revisiting of the two dozen years since Mom had given birth to me, it hit me: Like father, like daughter.

* * *

In late August of 1975, thirty months prior to the night of Mom's death, I had what I sincerely believed was my final conversation with Mom's father. Grandpa, a long-retired clergyperson, was battling serious medical complications. After a full decade of widowhood, he was now a resident of a nursing home in west Michigan.

Just days away from flying off to the Arabian Gulf state of Bahrain, where I was to serve as a mission volunteer, I had the opportunity to visit one last time with Grandpa. Sitting bedside with him, he and I held hands with familial intensity. Since my commitment to the work in Bahrain was for a minimum of nine months, he and I both understood this would be our last time in each other's earthly company. The likelihood of his survival for a full nine months was infinitesimal—and he made it clear he was ready to join Grandma, whom he missed profoundly. When our hour together drew to a close, we prayed quietly, hugged fiercely, shed tears unapologetically, and bade each other Godspeed.

A handful of days later I landed in Bahrain, where I remained for a full nine months. During that stretch of time I became an avid letter writer; phone calls were ponderously expensive, particularly given the minimal living expense budget I was understandably provided. Though Grandpa was unable to write to me, at least monthly I penned a short note for him, assuring him of my love and prayers. My mother, residing in northern New Jersey with Dad, kept me apprised of her father's health. Her reports suggested persistent decline. In fact, on at least two occasions during that winter of 1975–76, the nursing home staff called Mom on the east coast, informing her of Grandpa's fast approaching death. On both occasions she immediately headed for the airport in Newark, flew to Grand Rapids, and drove straight to the nursing home, an hour from the airport. In each instance, to the staff's surprise and my mother's confoundment, Grandpa rallied. He just would not "breathe his last."

Then, come early spring of 1976, the nursing home staff in Michigan once again phoned my mother in New Jersey. This time, though, it was to ask her a question. "Who might 'Bob' be, Mrs. Luidens?" the nurse inquired. "Your father keeps mumbling, 'Where's Bob?' When we ask him who he's referring to, we can't understand what he's saying." Mom reportedly responded with the suggestion it may be her son, Grandpa's grandson, who's on the other side of the planet in the Middle East. "Well," said the nurse, "his grandfather seems to want to see him."

I learned of the above in a letter my thoughtful mother mailed me in the weeks thereafter. She assured me I ought not be concerned by this peculiar, familial turn of events, but thought I might find it heartwarming to know. On reading that letter, I found myself welling up—with a tear in my eye and a pang in my heart.

In late May I finally flew westward from my Middle Eastern home in Bahrain to my old home in the odd world of New Jersey. Reunion with family, as well as with my soon-to-be fiancée, was pure delight. For the better part of two weeks, I began to settle back into the western world's flow—all the while knowing Grandpa was still alive more than six hundred miles away in west Michigan. My fiancée had graciously worked in the previous months to enable the two of us to serve as counselors in a summer church camp for children and youth in west Michigan beginning in late June. Were Grandpa to survive a few more weeks, I realized it was likely I would again have the chance to be in his company once I headed to Michigan for my summer job.

Then it happened. On Sunday, June 6, my parents and I came home from our New Jersey church. The phone rang shortly thereafter. Mom answered, and my father and I listened as she had a brief but serious conversation. Upon hanging up, she said, "Dad's dying. That was the nursing home staff." Mom and Dad then quietly agreed she should once again immediately drive to Newark Airport and grab a flight to Michigan.

In that moment, it hit me. "Mom," I said to both of them, "maybe I should go with you." Though I was already scheduled to fly out to Michigan within the next two weeks in order to start my summer job, going now seemed, well, right.

My parents looked at each other for a moment, and then both nodded. In unison. As if, for all practical purposes, each was sensing my going with Mom was essential. Even of design.

Our flight that evening had us touching down at the airport in Grand Rapids around ten p.m. Mom rented a car, and the two of us drove straight to the nursing home, arriving around thirty minutes before midnight. A staff person met us at the nursing home entryway, escorted us briskly to Grandpa's familiar room, and graciously closed the door behind us, leaving the three of us alone.

Grandpa was lying still in his bed, covers pulled up to his chin. He had lost at least fifty pounds since I had last been with him the previous August, when we had said "God be with you" to each other.

Mom went right to the head of the bed, pulled up a chair, and moved to just inches from Grandpa's hollowed out face. "Dad, we're here now. Bob and I just arrived from the airport." With that, standing on the opposite side of the bed from where Mom had sat down, I took Grandpa's hand, squeezed, and then knelt over him and kissed his forehead.

"Hi, Grandpa. It's Bob." No physical reaction seemed to come in response. But Mom held onto Grandpa's right hand, and I his left. There we were, one family, three generations, locked in familial affection and gratitude for all our little threesome embodied.

Then, to my utter astonishment, Grandpa's daughter began to speak in Dutch—a language I had never to that point ever heard Mom recite in any formal sense. Her phrasing betrayed the content. She first recited the Lord's Prayer. Then Psalm 23. Then she began to sing what later she explained to me were some psalms in Dutch her parents and grandparents had taught her when she was a little girl, half a century earlier.

To say that moment felt endearing would be understatement. It was in fact heavenly, suggestive not only of where it was Grandpa was soon heading, but of what had just broken into our hurting souls. All three of our souls.

For the better part of an hour Mom and I stayed bedside with Grandpa. Though a disinterested party might have suggested my grandfather was totally unaware of our presence, such an assessment would be, oh, entirely out of touch with reality.

My mother and I finally departed, after a quiet prayer—again in Dutch—lifted up quietly by Mom. She and I then drove fifteen minutes to a local hotel, checked into our room, and readied ourselves for a little sleep. Some fifteen minutes after we had tucked ourselves into our beds, the room's phone rang. It was the nursing home. The night charge nurse reported to Mom that Grandpa had just passed away.

* * *

Less than nineteen months after Grandpa's death in Michigan, I now lay in bed back in my New Jersey home. With *Mom's* death just hours earlier, my thoughts at four a.m. took me to countless places and memories. And among the flood of recollections was that of the phone call Mom had received in that hotel, informing her of Grandpa's death. A call that came, for all practical purposes, immediately after a reunion that Grandpa had somehow awaited for three quarters of a year.

"Like father, like daughter," I whispered to myself. Or more honestly, to our gracious maker—the one who had seen fit to bring Grandpa and

Mom and me into this mysterious world, and ultimately into the maker's one family.

Like father, like daughter—each having somehow played an active role in the one human moment over which one rarely thinks we have any control. Barring the exceptions of unspeakable tragedies embedded in suicide, execution, and warfare, the end of our mortal lives seems to the naked eye and the simplistic view to be entirely out of our control. Death comes when death comes, as so many poets and priests have intoned over the millennia. But somehow, in ways beyond human explanation, both Grandpa and Mom were insistent their last breath would not be spent until each had seen their heart's desire be met. For reasons that still leave me without words, Grandpa waited for his daughter and grandson. And Mom, like her father, waited for her children. Like father, like daughter.

Can I explain the above? No. Were I to be sworn in to give testimony in a court of law, attesting to a knowledge of the mystery of it all, would that testimony lead to a unanimous decision by a jury? I don't know—and I don't care. To the contrary, what matters still, almost a half century beyond those moments in Grandpa's and Mom's bedrooms, is that each in their moments received the gift for which they waited. The gift of family, embracing them with the same love *they* had given their entire, blessing-filled lives.

11

Hope

THE LOOK ON MY father's face was one I was unaccustomed to seeing. His expression was one of sadness, but also of peace. Maybe even of awe.

Less than a year following Mom's passing from cancer at the age of fifty-six, Dad and I were sitting in his quiet living room in New Jersey. I was visiting, taking a day away from my seminary classes in Connecticut, catching up with him as he was beginning to adjust to widowhood.

Just a handful of days earlier Dad had returned from another one of his exhausting, semi-annual, three week long treks to the other side of the globe. Those lengthy trips were part and parcel of his ministerial and administrative responsibilities as the National Council of Churches (U.S.A.) executive who related closely with churches throughout East Asia and the South Pacific. On this particular occasion he had visited with church leaders in Japan, South Korea, Taiwan, Hong Kong, the Philippines, Samoa, and Fiji. As had been the case on many previous such trips, he had returned home physically weary but spiritually renewed. That seemed once again to be the case as he and I sat together in his living room.

After we had a chance to catch up about any number of family-related issues, I asked him how the three weeks overseas had unfolded. That was when his face revealed that unexpected mix of sadness and peace. And even of awe.

"Well, Bob, something happened that still has me almost speechless." I nodded, and then he continued. "I had the chance to visit with two pastors, one in Seoul and the other in Manila. They were each in solitary confinement, and I was the first one to be allowed to see them in person in weeks, if not months." That's when his eyes began to water a bit. But with those tears came the hint of a smile. I realized in that moment I was about to hear something unique. Even divine.

A bit of background. The year was 1978. For well more than a decade both South Korea and the Philippines had been led by dictatorial leaders. Park Chung-hee was the army general who ruled South Korea with martial law ferocity in Seoul. Similarly, Ferdinand Marcos was the iron-fisted president in Manila. Though their rules would inevitably come to incendiary ends in the next few years, their domination of their countries' citizens was currently uncompromising and cruel.

As I had learned from my father in the previous few years, many churches in both nations had become settings of vocal objection to their countries' autocratic rule. A growing number of pastors, to their inestimable credit, had begun to preach from their pulpits about the God-given rights of their homelands' citizenry that were being repressed beyond measure. In due course, both Park and Marcos opted to suppress those prophetic voices. A Korean Presbyterian minister was summarily arrested by Park's military police, and then imprisoned in solitary confinement. Likewise, a Filipino Catholic priest was taken into custody and ultimately sequestered in solitary confinement. In both instances, as Dad learned, they were allowed virtually no visitors.

Feeling compelled to express America's objection to this unjust treatment of these two clergypersons, Dad communicated with the State Department in Washington, D.C. Given the enormous military and economic support the U.S. was providing to both South Korea and the Philippines at the time, as well as President Jimmy Carter's stated commitment to human rights, Dad managed to secure from the State Department two letters. One was addressed to President Park's regime, the other to President Marcos's. In each instance the letter requested in firm terms that my father was to be allowed access to each prisoner.

Dad had then flown across the Pacific. Upon arriving in Seoul, he communicated with the appropriate government officials, presenting his letter from the State Department. In due course, under the watchful, distrusting eye of Korean intelligence operatives, my father was allowed entry into the prison where the Presbyterian minister was in solitary confinement. Likewise, a week later he was led into the holding cell of the Catholic priest in his Manila prison. In both instances, he visited one-on-one with the prisoner, conveying to each the deep, prayerful concern and support of their Christian sisters and brothers in the U.S.

As Dad and I now sat in his living room, not more than a handful of days since he had been able to embody that pastoral presence in the prison cells of those two ministers, Dad began to describe for me a bit of the two conversations he had had with them. Each of the men, he said, was understandably lonely. They missed their loved ones. They yearned to be reunited with their parishioners. And they were sincerely moved to have this previously unknown minister from the U.S. now sitting with them, assuring them they were not forgotten.

But then my father's eyes began to water a bit. And that trace of a smile began to show. "Bob," he said, "it's what then happened in both of those solitary confinement cells that I want to tell you about." I remember getting a bit of a chill, not knowing at all what he was going to disclose.

"What, Dad?"

Looking over my shoulder, not at the living room wall, but well beyond, he said, "Each of them told me what he had begun to experience." I nodded. And waited. Then: "Each of them told me he had begun to experience hope. *Hope*. In fact, each of them told me he had begun to realize he had never before reflected on hope in as real a way as he was doing there in solitary confinement." Then he looked me in the eye and said, "And each of them told me he was beginning to write. About a theology of hope. About how God was with him in a way he'd never yet experienced out in the wider world. Each of them told me he was feeling in his bones and in his heart that God was there, with him, in as undeniable a way as he'd ever felt to that point in his life. And that God would never, ever leave him. No matter what."

Dad stopped. I waited for him to continue. After a meaningful silence, he said, "And neither of them knew anything about the other. How *could* they have?" Again the tears and the smile. "I just happened to be the fortunate one to receive this priceless gift of both men telling me about hope in the most hopeless settings imaginable."

I confess I don't recall how I responded to Dad's words. But I do remember how I felt. I was moved beyond measure. I was touched with both a sense of peace and a surge of passion. Those two men, who had never met and were as isolated as anyone could ever be, were clearly, indisputably embraced by the same divine. They were each clothed with a matchless, spirit-nourishing gift: hope. Not the kind one may feel in ordinary circumstances. No, the kind that is rooted in the extraordinary. In the eternal.

I've thought about that quiet exchange in my father's living room on any number of occasions. Each time I do, the memory stirs me. It awakens me. Actually, I confess it re-births hope within *me*.

Could it be our God gives to us the gift of hope when we least expect it, but most need it? My dear father's experience in those two cells, with those two brothers in Christ, argues just that.

I, for one, couldn't ask for a more priceless gift.

12

With Feet of Clay

BEFORE I DID MY usual thing of carefully crafting my words, I smiled, looked for a moment at the ceiling, and said simply, "Mom *wasn't* perfect, was she."

The year was 1979. My wife and I, both now twenty-six years old, were living in Ann Arbor. Mary was in her fourth and final year of medical school. Meanwhile, having completed my first two years of seminary, I was in the second of two years of ministry internship six hundred miles west of my seminary's campus. The first of those two years I had served as a student ministry staff member with a wonderful congregation sitting adjacent to the university campus. The second year saw me now embedded with the chaplaincy program of that university's esteemed medical center.

My hands-on chaplaincy learning experience was coordinated by the medical center's chief of chaplains. Herb was in his late sixties, a nationally renowned co-designer of what is widely respected as Clinical Pastoral Education. He was a fascinating mix of both disarming joviality and brutal honesty. Each morning, Monday through Friday, the four of us student chaplains would enter as a group into Herb's quiet office for an intense two hours of conversation with him. Herb demanded of all four of us absolute honesty about our experiences on the various hospital units to which he would assign us to give pastoral care to patients. From one morning to the next, all four of us student chaplains would share, sometimes in jolting, tear-filled detail, what we were discovering about ourselves in the midst of our daily engagement with patients and their loved ones.

Somewhere around the fifth or sixth week of our nine months of that student chaplaincy training with Herb, he instructed all four of us that we were each to find a therapeutic counselor. He explained it was imperative we explore, in the safety of the confidentiality that professional therapy entails, what some of our own personal issues might be. "If you don't honestly discover, name, and address those issues," explained Herb, "they're bound silently but corrosively to impact your ministry with your patients now, and with your parishioners in the future, if you end up in parish ministry. Those patients and parishioners deserve pastors who *know* themselves, clay feet and all."

Well more than four decades later, I remain immeasurably embarrassed to confess I chuckled quietly to myself when Herb instructed all of us to find a personal therapist. At the same time as I stupidly nodded in solemn agreement with him, I was thinking arrogantly, "Like *I* need a therapist. Please." In time I discovered all three of my student chaplain peers in Herb's office that morning were privately duplicating my reaction. And I suspect—no, I'm sure—Herb knew it.

Two weeks later I sat for the first time in the comfortable office of the Rev. Dr. Curtis Appleton. Curt, as he kindly invited me to address him, was a sixty year old therapist whose name had been on the list of recommended counselors Herb had given to all four us. As his title suggested, Curt was both an ordained clergyperson and the recipient of a doctorate in clinical psychology. He had served as a parish pastor for almost twenty years, and then had pursued his PhD. Now into his second decade of therapeutic counseling, he exuded both gentility and thoughtfulness. Within the first few minutes of meeting him I felt warmly received and in safe company.

Looking down at the intake notes I had provided him prior to our first session together, Curt said, "So, Bob, your information here indicates you were instructed by Herb to engage in some extended therapy during the next seven months while you serve as a student chaplain." When I nodded, he continued. "Well, as a way of getting started together, how about if you give me some idea of what you feel might be helpful for the two of us to discuss going forward."

I confess I sat there for a moment, wordless. In my case, that was out of the ordinary. But in due course I responded, "Well, Curt, I'm not really sure *what* would be helpful to talk about with you. I feel I have a pretty good handle on myself, and don't know of any real issues I need to work on." Even today I still blanch when I revisit that astonishing disclosure of absolute unawareness of my inner life. But at least I was being honest. I truly was disconnected from—blind and deaf to—dynamics in my young life that had left significant, sometimes painful imprint on my mind and soul.

Patient and evocative therapist that he was, Curt nodded. While he had every reason to guffaw in disbelief at my unadulterated self-ignorance, he didn't. Instead, bless him, he said, "Okay. Then how about this: why don't you tell me about your life story. Maybe you can start with your memories of growing up—where you've lived, some things about your parents, your siblings, if you have any. And we can go from there."

I'm sure I nodded at that suggestion. "That works," I probably said. "That I can do." And with that I dove in. I recall describing my being born to two amazing parents, who had served as missionaries in the Middle East before and after my birth. After a brief introduction to my two older siblings, I returned to Mom and Dad. Somewhere in those first few minutes, I noted that twenty months earlier my "saint of a mother" had died at age fifty-six after battling cancer for several years. Curt kindly conveyed his condolences to me, and then invited me to tell him a little more about Mom. "Well, she was perfect, Curt." Remarkably he didn't interrupt at that staggering assessment. Instead, he let me proceed. "She was always loving. I could always talk to her about anything. Since Dad traveled extensively and would be gone for days, and sometimes multiple weeks at a time, she was the one who was in charge of our home. She really was perfect."

And so it went. For the next two, maybe three sessions, I regaled Curt with all things affirmative about my childhood, especially about my loving parents. I did so at great length. Until the moment when I stumbled for a short but not insignificant second or two.

I was describing incidental recollections from my childhood school years. On the thirtieth of October in my seventh year, I noted to Curt, Mom invited me to accompany her to a specialty store that sold Halloween costumes. Excited about the trick or treating in our New Jerssey neighborhood the next day, we browsed the store's many options. I finally settled on an orange pumpkin that had a smiling face imprinted on its front. Mom nodded her agreement this costume fit the bill. She took a plastic packaged pumpkin outfit to the counter, paid for it, then drove us homeward. The whole way I jabbered about my growing eagerness to roam from house to house the following day, proudly representing all Halloween gourds.

But then, I explained to Curt, the next afternoon arrived. Having rushed home from school, I raced up the stairs to my bedroom where the package lay on my bed, awaiting my donning of the pumpkin for the ensuing trick or treat adventure. Mom followed me upstairs, watching from the bedroom door with delight on her face as I ripped open the package, pulling out the cloth costume. Fumbling with the arm holes, I managed to pull it over my head. I then headed over to the mirrored closet door for a full inspection. But when I did so, my jaw went slack. As did my mother's. The costume, rather than puff out fittingly to resemble a plump pumpkin, flopped to the floor, with half of the gourd piled around my little feet. Mom came close, stroked my head in order to settle me for a moment, and then checked the size marker on the back of the costume's neck. "Uh-oh," she mumbled.

"What, Mom?" I asked, still gawking at myself in the mirror.

"Uh, it's the wrong size, I'm afraid."

"Whadda you mean?"

"It's a size sixteen. Not a six," she said, shaking her head with resignation. "I thought I saw the number 'six' when I took it to the cashier. But it's a sixteen."

In retrospect, the sight in the mirror was worthy of a Halloween cackle. With the drooping pumpkin smile, and the oversized cloth flowing around my skinny shoulders all the way to the floor, I likely looked something akin to a juvenile rendering of Edvard Munch's iconic painting entitled "The Scream." In fact, had my beloved mother not embraced me warmly at that very moment, I would likely have, well, screamed myself.

It was while describing to Curt this utterly benign, comical moment from my childhood, I stopped. Curt let me sit quietly as I pondered the simple but significant truth embedded in my account. Before I did my usual thing of carefully crafting my words, I smiled, looked for a moment at the ceiling, and said simply, "Mom *wasn't* perfect, was she."

Curt let me sit quietly in the ensuing silence. It was then, having tripped over the absurd fantasy of Mom's "perfection," I looked at Curt. It was as though I needed him to help me back up from where I had just stumbled. "Tell me, Bob," Curt said gently, lifting me up ever so slowly.

I continued to smile, shaking my head at my own disconnect from reality. "I've never let my mother be anything but a perfect person. But she wasn't." And I didn't need to add, "And not just with how well she shopped for Halloween costumes." After another moment of headshaking and thought, I confess to saying one more time, "Mom *wasn't* perfect."

Whereas Curt could have said, "Of course she wasn't," he didn't. Instead he said quietly, "Maybe we can start again to talk about your real mother. And about yourself." He didn't add "more honestly." He didn't need to. I now knew it, in the bone of my bones. I needed to reimagine who my late mother was, in fairness both to her and to myself. And I needed especially to discover who I was, in fairness to myself and to everyone with whom I would share my unfolding life.

That was when I realized I needed to explore, with unfettered honesty, my real life story. Who I really am. Were I not to allow myself the work—the important privilege—of honest self-discovery, I would be not only of potential harm to myself. I might be less than helpful to everyone around me. That included patients in the medical center that year in Ann Arbor. And that would include any number of parishioners in two congregations over the next four decades.

Since 1979 I have therefore chosen to spend countless hours with at least seven different counseling therapists. Most have been enormously helpful. But each has had his or her own unique style. By way of example, there was Dr. Norton. Dr. Norton, whom I was absolutely *not* invited to address by his first name, engaged me in a manner one hundred and eighty degrees differently than Curt.

Dr. Norton was a psychologist on the staff of Yale University's medical school. Remarkably, he and his peers were available free of charge to those of us who were studying at Yale's seminary, the Divinity School. On returning from Ann Arbor to New Haven for my final year in seminary, following my several months of counseling with Curt, I made an appointment to see one of Yale's therapists. I was informed Dr. Norton would fill that role.

On the appointed day and time, I arrived at Yale's student counseling center. Though intensely quiet, there sat a dozen of us students waiting to see our assigned counselors. After sitting for a few minutes, looking forward to meeting my new "Curt," a secretary silently escorted me down a long hallway. She pointed at a door with a "Dr. Norton" placard hanging on it, and said rather perfunctorily, "In there." She then turned and walked away without another word.

I stood in front of the door, unsure how to proceed. I finally knocked once. I then heard a stern, "Come." I tentatively turned the knob, pushed the door open halfway, put my head around the edge of the door, and beheld a man sitting sternly behind a desk, staring deadeye at me.

"Dr. Norton?" I asked tentatively. He nodded, but said nothing. "May I come in?"

He nodded again, his face betraying no emotion.

I walked into the drab, undecorated office, closing the door as quietly as possible behind me. Other than Dr. Norton's desk, the only furniture was a hard, straight back chair facing that desk. Nothing else. Feeling unsure what to do or say, I stood behind the chair for a moment or two, looking at him. "Shall I sit?" I asked, now feeling a chill course through my torso. He shrugged, saying not one word. I took the shrug to mean, "Of course, I'd be *delighted* to have you join me in warm conversation!" Well, actually not. I took the shrug to suggest unmitigated inhospitality. And even that may be understating the frigidity of the moment.

So I sat. Once in my chair, we found ourselves facing each other straight on. He looked at me wordlessly. To that point all I had heard him say was "Come." Probably fidgeting by now, I did what he likely anticipated I would do. I spoke. "Thank you for letting me come to see you." No response.

I fidgeted all the more. Finally, after another five or ten seconds of absolute stillness, I ventured, "Is there anything you'd like me to say?"

To which he responded coldly, "Why do you need me to tell you what to say?"

That was it. For a moment I didn't know how to respond. Because I didn't really know the answer to his fitting, albeit callous-sounding question. "I guess I don't know why I need you to tell me what to say. I figured you're the counselor and would ask me to tell you about myself." He continued to stare at me, saying not one additional word. "Is there anything you'd like me to talk about?"

He said, "Why do you need me to tell you what to talk about?" I then fell silent, totally unsure how to answer. Or how to proceed. I contemplated standing and leaving the frigid field of battle as fast as possible. But I stayed, realizing I was somehow at a new point in my life. Somehow in a moment of opportunity—frightening as it felt—to further discover who I was. Who I am.

"I guess I wasn't *aware* of my needing you to tell me what to say, Dr. Norton." He nodded.

"What were you thinking would happen in this office?" he asked, still fairly hard in tone.

"I'm not entirely sure. I think I was expecting—or hoping—I'd be able to be in the company of a supportive therapist who would help me explore myself."

"Why do you need someone who's supportive?" he asked.

I thought for a moment, and then said, "That's what I had out in Ann Arbor. My therapist back there was overtly supportive. Emotionally encouraging."

In retrospect I think I actually believed my words would break the ice, inviting Dr. Norton to say, "Oh, well then I'll gladly be your new Curt." But he did no such thing. Instead, he said, "Why do you need me to be emotionally encouraging?"

Again the silence, uncertain how to respond. Finally: "I'm not sure. I guess I need someone to help me feel encouraged."

"You need someone *else* to do that for you? And you're planning to be a pastor in the near future?" he then asked, quietly but sternly. When I didn't respond, maybe because I didn't need to provide the obvious answer, he said, "*Now* we have something to talk about, do we not?"

Seven months later, I had my twentieth and final session with Dr. Norton. We didn't embrace, nor did we express any artificial hope of reunion in the future. But I departed with a far deeper awareness of, among many issues, my burdensome need for approval from others—a need, time and time again since then, I've had to confront and address. Dr. Norton's therapeutic approach, so totally at odds with that of Curt, is one through which I learned to practice more honest, and at times taxing, self-examination.

In similar ways, each of the various opportunities for me to engage in widely differing therapeutic conversations has given me a means to discover—to acknowledge—who I really am. How I am so fully human. How, as Herb had said, I truly have feet of clay.

13

Omniscience

IT'S BEEN WELL MORE than four decades since that car ride home with my father. But I can still recall our exchange with startling clarity. "So you're saying this evening was no comparison to what you went through back then?" I asked him.

"No," he smiled graciously, "no comparison at all." He was behind the wheel, but he glanced over at me with a gentle, if not wry, smile. "None whatsoever."

It happened to be my twenty-eighth birthday. That evening I had just sat through my final oral examination for preparedness to be ordained into the office of Minister of Word and Sacrament. Earlier that month I had graduated from seminary, having completed five years of post-college training. Three of those years had been on campus, and the other two doing pastoral ministry training in a church parish and a large medical center. Now with those years of academic and practical experience under my belt, I had just sat through two hours of questioning by members of the governing church body who oversaw some twenty local congregations in New Jersey, including the one of which I had been a member since age eleven.

The oral questioning that evening had been not only of me, but of three others who had also just completed theological training and were anticipating possible ordination as pastors. The four of us had sat side by side in chairs on the elevated chancel of a church sanctuary, facing some sixty women and men whose responsibility it was to determine whether or not each of us was fit for the demanding responsibilities that lay ahead if and when we were to receive congregational "calls"—job offers, in everyday parlance.

I had anticipated those two hours to be stressful. Coming into the evening, I had presumed there would be a host of demanding questions posed to the four of us, each intended to unveil any number of shortcomings one or another of us might have. If the intent of the examination was to ensure each of us was truly ready to begin serving as a responsible minister, I had figured this to be the final testing moment—the last opportunity to prevent any unfit pastor-wannabe from moving into a position of significant responsibility and ending up failing in doing so. Such failure could be devastating both to that individual, as well as to the congregation amongst whom she or he would do the failing.

But my anticipation about the two hours of questioning proved wrong. Rather than being assaulted by a host of challenging questions, the four of us sitting up front were invited to answer some of the simplest, least demanding queries I could have imagined. "What are the names of the four Gospels?" "How many commandments did God give to the Israelites through Moses?" "What are the elements used during the sacrament of Communion?" By minute one hundred and twenty, all such softball questions had been hammered out of the ecclesiastical ball park by all four of us. After ten minutes of then being excused from the sanctuary, the four of us were ushered back in and told we were all affirmed for ordination. Applause was given. After a warm prayer and benediction, the whole assembly moved into the church's fellowship hall and enjoyed some cookies and cider. Thereafter we all headed to the church parking lot and began driving to our respective homes. That included my dear father and me.

Dad had sat silently in the back pew of the sanctuary for that evening's examination. Though an ordained minister himself, he was not a member of this particular governing church body, so had not been afforded a part in the questioning. But he had observed very carefully, as I soon learned.

Two minutes after he and I had begun our short drive from the examination site back to his home, I ventured a question. "So, Dad, did this evening bring back any memories?"

"It certainly did," he responded. "But not in the way you might guess."

"How so?" I asked.

"Well, what you just went through was hardly comparable to what I endured when I went through my ordination exams."

"You're saying this evening was no comparison to what you went through back then?"

"No," he smiled graciously, "no comparison at all." He glanced over at me with a gentle, if not wry, smile. "None whatsoever."

On my invitation, my father then explained. He described how he had been examined with Peter, a fellow seminary graduate who ended up being his lifelong friend ever since their shared examination experience back in 1943. The two of them had sat in front of more than one hundred adults from eight a.m. until five p.m., with only a brief break at noon for lunch. Their exam entailed eight separate topical emphases, each consuming a full hour of questioning. Greek took an hour. Sacramental theology took an hour. Old Testament took an hour. And so forth. During each of those hours of oral questioning, examining the two of them was *the* member of the gathered assembly who was considered the most adept at that hour's assigned focus. "So," Dad said, "old Pastor Vander Kolk grilled us on Paul's letters, because everyone knew that was his special expertise. And scholarly Elder Brookman, who taught European history in a nearby university, pressed us on all things having to do with the Reformation." Staring straight ahead at the dark road on which he and I were driving homeward, Dad then said, "By the time the eight hours were over, Peter and I stumbled out of the sanctuary and were totally convinced we had failed the overall examination. During each of those hourlong segments, there were countless times when neither of us had any clue how to answer a question. I don't know how many times he and I said, somewhat sheepishly, 'I'm sorry, but I don't know.'"

"So what happened, Dad?" I asked, sincerely curious.

"Well, after a half hour of anxiously pacing out in the waiting area, Peter and I were called back into the sanctuary. We were pointed back to our two chairs in front of everyone. There was absolute silence in the sanctuary. Then the presiding officer informed us that our examinations had been sustained." I looked at Dad in the dark interior of our car, uncertain what he meant. "They had passed us, with commendation."

"Seriously?"

"Yes," Dad said. "Then Peter and I were told this by the presiding officer. 'Peter and Edwin, we have voted unanimously to affirm your preparedness to be ordained as Ministers of Word and Sacrament. But you now can well appreciate this: neither of you knows everything. Though you've each clearly done exceptionally well in your three years of academic work in seminary, there is so, so much that you have yet to learn. That was, and is, the case for everyone coming out of seminary. In fact, that's the case especially for those of us who have been in ministry for more than half a century. None of us knows it all. To the contrary, we are each and all called to be learners for the rest of our earthly lives. Our parishioners deserve nothing less.'"

By the time my father and I had pulled into the driveway, it was crystal clear what Dad wanted me to understand. I had just "endured" two hours of testing that in no way challenged the four of us sitting up front that evening. We had passed our examination, but had not been afforded the humbling opportunity to be reminded that being prepared for ministry did not equate with knowing everything—with being an unquestionable expert. To the contrary, we had been allowed to leave the gathering with the dangerous presumption of expertise. With the unhelpful—even destructive—attitude of omniscience. My father, in retrospect, wanted me to know what Peter and he had had to confront thirty-eight years earlier: that each and every one of us has unboundedly more yet to learn.

That car ride lesson took root. Over the years since then I have frequently found myself given supervisory responsibility over seminary students as they, too, prepare for possible ordination into ministry. In each of those circumstances I've made the effort to ensure that every one of them would have the opportunity to know both that they are supported in their academic and professional preparations, *and* that they do not yet—nor ever will in this earthly life—know it all.

Sadly, too frequently over recent decades I have found myself witness to instances of individuals betraying a destructive, hubris-filled conviction of omniscience—believing they know more than others, and even that they know the absolute truth. Such moments have unfolded in church settings, including Sunday sermons. But they have been on display, as well, in academic lectures and media punditry, at political rallies and town hall meetings, and from congressional committees and Supreme Court benches. The corrosive impact of those instances is incalculable.

In my humbled estimation, along with that of Dad and so many other wonderful mentors I've been blessed to know over the decades, no pastor—no person—should *ever* presume omniscience. Such is the domain of our gracious Lord alone.

14

Pressure

It was my first formal interview with any pastoral search committee. But even then I knew it was—and would remain—as strange as any I could ever imagine.

It all started several years earlier. Back then my wife and I were midstream in our advanced academic training, she in medical school and I in seminary. Near the start of her third year, Mary and her medical school classmates learned of an intriguing invitation. It was from the U.S. government's National Health Service (NHS). The NHS was offering substantial financial assistance to any future physicians willing to commit to provide service in a medically underserved area once having completed at least one year of internship subsequent to receiving their medical degree. After some extensive discussion, and no small measure of prayer, Mary and I agreed that the NHS offer was intriguing, and even appealing. She made the commitment.

Two and a half years later Mary was midway through her internship year and I was well into my final year of seminary. As anticipated, communication began with the NHS. Mary received from the NHS a list of several communities in the Midwest who were looking for physicians to fill significant voids in their medical service. One was the farming community of Lincoln County in north-central Kansas. Seven hundred and twenty square miles in size, the county's population was around four thousand, with the county seat of Lincoln itself home to around sixteen hundred residents. That town of Lincoln boasted an established hospital with some dozen beds, as well as an attached, busy out-patient clinic that provided a breadth of medical care for patients of all ages. At the time, only one physician resided in the entire county. Understandably, the hospital's medical board—as well as the whole community—were eager, if not desperate, to recruit at least one other physician to help provide the county's vast array of medical services.

The possibility of serving in Lincoln began to appeal to both Mary and me. She communicated her willingness to visit the county and meet in person with the medical staff, their one physician, and the hospital's board. In the meantime, to our delight we discovered there was a small Presbyterian congregation in Lincoln who were searching for their next pastor. Examining the search committee's informational packet, I found myself drawn to communicate my willingness to meet in person with them, optimally at the same time as Mary would meet with the hospital's leadership. Happily all parties agreed to make it happen.

In due course Mary and I flew from Connecticut out to the Midwest, and drove into Lincoln, arriving at noon. We walked into one of the town's little eateries—the Chew 'n Chat—and enjoyed a sandwich. By the time we arrived at the hospital around two o'clock for some preliminary touring of the medical facilities, the staff already knew we were in town. Unbeknownst to the two of us, folks at the Chew 'n Chat had sent word ahead.

The afternoon unfolded auspiciously. We enjoyed warm conversations with the county's one physician, the hospital and clinic nurses, and the director of the hospital. A driving tour gave us a firsthand look at the town and surrounding farmland.

Then it was time for supper. But this was no ordinary mealtime, much less collection of diners. The evening meal was kindly hosted by the hospital board in the staff dining hall. But it was the diverse collection of diners that was striking. Those present were not only the medical staff, extending a warm welcome to Mary. Those around the large square set-up of tables also included the five members of the Presbyterian Church's pastoral search committee.

I had earlier communicated fairly extensively by letter and phone with the pastoral search committee's chairperson. Jack had graciously agreed to schedule my full meeting with the search committee that same evening after supper. While Mary would have serious conversation with the medical board at the hospital, I would contemporaneously meet with the search committee at the church. To my mild surprise, the five members of the search committee had been invited to be part of the supper gathering in the hospital's staff dining hall. I was briefly introduced to all five as we took our seats at the large square of tables, but conversation with them was impeded by the understandable engagement—well, excited wooing—by the board members with my dear, patient wife. What was quickly evident to all fifteen to twenty of us around the tables was that everything imaginable was being done and said in order to convince Mary to accept their invitation to become their county's second physician in residence.

Meanwhile, there I sat in close proximity to the five pastoral search committee members, who in turn sat in relative silence, observing the barely disguised desperation of the medical board members doing whatever they could to land their county's next doctor. To say it was unusual, if not uncomfortable, would be understatement.

Finally the agreed upon hour of seven o'clock arrived. With dessert dishes cleared away, all rose from our seats. While Mary remained with the medical folks, I headed off to the nearby church building in a six car procession. Once parked in front of the church, the five search committee members and I took a quiet tour of the building, and then headed into a small conference room. Chairperson Jack invited me to sit at the head of the table, with the five of them sitting to my right and left.

Jack kindly suggested I open our conversation with prayer. After I did so, we sat in awkward silence for five seconds, maybe ten. Jack then said, fairly awkwardly, "Well, here we are." He looked around at the other four, who shuffled their feet in a surprisingly embarrassed manner. One of them coughed, not so much to clear her throat as to suggest an apparent sense of unease.

That's when it hit me, although I had begun to wonder about it during the previous two hours of mealtime back at the hospital. "Jack," I began, "maybe it would be good—even helpful—if we took a moment to process what the six of us just went through since five o'clock this evening." Though such a suggestion may rightly be called peculiar, if not unscripted, it immediately struck a chord. All five of the committee members to my right and left nodded vigorously, both at one another and at me. The body language was definitive. It was as though my suggestion invited the release of their pent-up angst, with all five now seemingly desperate to talk.

"Bob, that's a great idea," responded Jack. Nods all around the table. But still no one uttered another word.

Which is when I asked, "I presume you folks were all invited by the hospital board to the dinner where my wife had the red carpet rolled out for her?" Again the nods. "Is it fair to presume you were expected to make both Mary and me feel warmly welcome?" Nods upon nods. "That makes sense, given how much your county's residents really need another doctor."

Nellie, to my right, responded. "We all want another doc in town, Bob. So we understand the board's urgency." She stopped, looking around at her four compatriots. It was as though she wanted to say something else, along with all four of the others, but just couldn't bring herself to do so.

After another few seconds of silence, I ventured where earlier I had no anticipation of having to go. "I guess I need to ask the five of you an awkward question." They all stared at me with expressions that betrayed desperation. "Were any of you given the impression you had better offer me the promise of a call to be your next pastor?"

With that question, there was an expulsion of air that almost took *my* breath away. All five nodded with vigor. Eyes bulged and shoulders slumped. "Yes!" said Bernice, sitting opposite Nellie. "Yes! I've had countless people come up to me and whisper, 'We're counting on you five to do what's right. We all need a doctor, so you'd do well to make sure the doctor's husband becomes your next pastor.'"

"I even get pressure from my wife," chimed in Jack. "It's been, well, really tense."

Over the next several minutes the previously silent committee of five evolved into a talkative, transparent circle. I simply listened, allowing them to process together—in my presence—what their experiences had been like for the previous couple of weeks. Clearly they had endured a kind of pressure none of them had any reason to anticipate when, many months earlier, they had agreed to serve on the search committee.

When all five had finally shared their experiences and had released their pent-up anxiety, I discerned it was time for me to comment. Or more to the point, to reassure. "Folks, I sincerely appreciate your so honestly sharing with me what it's been like to be under this odd pressure from some folks in the wider community to make sure you offer me the call to be your congregation's next pastor. But I want to assure you," I said, looking each one of them in the eye, "I sincerely trust God will make God's will known to you *and* to Mary and me. And I sincerely believe God will provide for you, as well as for the congregation and the whole community, even if I'm not meant to be your next pastor."

All five nodded, this time more slowly than earlier. But each then smiled quietly, as well. It was as though they were allowing themselves to throw off the burden of making the wider community happy, and were instead recommitting themselves to the appropriate task at hand: discerning God's will, not that of their neighbors, nor even of their spouses.

I confess I don't know the answer to the following question. Was my asking them about the pressure they were experiencing over the previous days and weeks a significant factor in their discernment about my potentially becoming their next pastor? Maybe, or maybe not. Regardless, it was a question that quite evidently needed to be asked.

Within the next few days Mary and I flew home to Connecticut. The Lincoln hospital board then graciously offered her the position of physician on staff. And the Presbyterian Church's pastoral search committee informed me they were eagerly prepared to present my name to the church's governing board if I were prepared to accept a call to be their next pastor.

Mary and I joyfully accepted both.

Ultimately we remained in service in Lincoln for three years, extending beyond the two years of commitment Mary had originally made to the NHS. They were wonderful years, for which we have been humbly grateful ever since.

But the Lincoln story doesn't end there.

Some forty months after that transformative, first meeting with the pastoral search committee, I announced from the pulpit at the close of a Sunday morning worship hour that Mary and I had accepted positions in upstate New York in a medical center and a congregation, respectively. We would be moving back east within the month. As I shared those words I found myself tearing up, if not almost sobbing, so deep was the affection Mary and I had developed for the congregation and the whole county's populace.

The next morning while working at my desk at church, the phone started ringing. Within the next forty-eight hours, at least half a dozen members of the congregation called to schedule one-on-one visits with me. Those conversations unfolded, but not in the way I anticipated. Whereas I had prepared myself for any number of church members beseeching their pastor not to abandon them, I received a very different appeal. Every single one of the dear parishioners who came to see me in my study wondered aloud, "How are we ever going to manage without Dr. Mary?"

If memory serves, those making that heartfelt appeal included both Jack and Nellie.

15

Friends

Maybe it was true for Avery. But as the years unfolded, I confess it wasn't true for me.

Avery was a fellow pastor of a different denomination than my own, and one with two dozen more years under his clerical belt than I. He had graciously invited me out for lunch just two weeks after my wife and I had arrived in the wonderful farming community where we were just beginning our fulltime vocations as physician and pastor. Knowing I had completed my theological training just three months earlier, Avery now saw fit to assist me with the myriad adjustments necessary to make the transition from student to pastor.

While the two of us first began chatting informally about the impending wheat harvest our two congregations' parishioners were anticipating any day now, a friendly waitress arrived and placed mammoth BLT sandwich plates in front of each of us, accompanied with a pleasant "Enjoy." Avery immediately bowed his head. Without warning he began to pray—for God's blessing on the meal, but also on me.

Once he had intoned a fittingly serious "Amen," he started in. While I chowed down on the scrumptious sandwich—whose pork likely had been living and breathing not more than forty-eight hours earlier, given its glorious flavor—he began to enumerate any number of things he discerned important for the newbie minister to keep in mind as I began serving my congregation and the wider community. "You'll want to be sure to plan on at least one day each week when you leave work behind. Don't go to the church building on that day, if at all possible. And you might want to avoid the post office, as well." While chewing and nodding in silence, I listened to additional counsel, unsolicited but proffered nonetheless. "Keep a small spiral notebook in the glove compartment. You'll need to record every mile you drive if you're going to be able to claim your actual travel expenses on your income tax returns. And don't forget to record those miles to the tenth." When I stared at him with a look of confusion, he clarified. "You know. If you drive 6.2 miles, don't write down '6.' Mark down '6.2.' Those tenths add up over the course of twelve months." When I nodded my understanding, he continued apace.

Avery's expansive advice, although unsolicited, proved of interest. I made mental note of a host of his suggestions, most all of which seemed to make sense to my inexperienced soul. But in the midst of all his recommendations that noon was one I found myself repeatedly hearkening back to over the years. I did so because my experience began to suggest his urging was misguided, if not wrong. "Bob," Avery said, "one thing you'll figure out has to do with friendship. You'll find you'll not want to be friends with your parishioners. Instead, you'll find all the friends you need among your fellow pastors. It's safer that way." When I nodded, crunching on a potato chip, he continued. "You see, your parishioners will be fine folks and all. But you won't be able to trust them to be your friends. That's where other ministers will fit in. They'll understand you. And they'll stand by you, especially whenever you may have a conflict with some of your congregation's members." With that, Avery moved on to some other bit of advice about how to make sure the church sexton never goes through the waste basket in my study and finds embarrassing papers. "Make sure you tear up those sheets into small bits," he said, with a wink and a smile. So it went during that lunch time together some four decades ago.

But the months and years of ministry then unfolded. And with the passing of that time, it was Avery's strong urging about friends that repeatedly came into question for me.

Implicit in Avery's advice was a combination of suppositions I found less and less true to my experience. As the years added up, new and lasting friendships were indeed birthed in my life—but more often than not they were with members of the congregations I served as pastor. While some friendships with fellow clergy were also taking shape—and indeed deeply so in a handful of instances—more often than not those with whom I found myself in profoundly warm, honest relationship were my parishioners. And fascinatingly, I realized, those friendships were with folks who were incredibly diverse. Some of those whom I began seriously to call "friend" were highly educated professionals, serving in education, various sciences, and the law. But just as frequently, some were high school graduates at best, now engaged in community service as plumbers, farmers, and grocers. Some worked full time at home, while others part-time in preschools, non-profits, and community service agencies. A great many were retired, now engaged in volunteer work in extraordinary ways. And a host of my *dearest* friends were residents of assisted living facilities and nursing homes, soul-stirringly ready to ponder aloud with me about the endless mysteries of this human pilgrimage.

While it was certainly the case that some elements of my ministry responsibilities and challenges were best discussed with fellow pastors, I found repeatedly that wider concerns were just as beneficially pursued with those who had no theological training whatsoever. It was with members of my congregations, as well as of other nearby parishes, I learned the rich blessings of Christlike character during a limitless variety of discussions. It was with my non-pastor friends I was witness again and again to humility and honesty. It was with my parishioners I saw displayed a rejection of criticism and competition, and an embrace of vision and vulnerability.

All these years later I've found myself wondering what a follow-up lunch conversation with Avery might elicit. I suspect he might still be an advocate for the counsel he offered me about limiting one's friendships to the elitist circle of ordained clergy. Or maybe not. It's possible in his later years he, too, may have allowed himself the unspeakable wealth of camaraderie with lay people in his pews, over against solely with those preaching in other pulpits. Regardless, the years since I enjoyed that luscious BLT sandwich in his company have proven beyond any wisp of doubt that my parishioners have comprised the vast majority of my friends. For that I am eternally grateful.

16

Only Silence

Sybil responded, "Yes, Pastor Bob, that *is* what I suggest."

I probably blinked a bit of disbelief, if not disagreement. But she was the musician; I most certainly was not. And she had been on this Lenten pilgrimage far, far longer than me. "Well, okay. Then let's not have any music played whatsoever during the Maundy Thursday service's time of Communion." She nodded wordlessly, clearly grateful the young, inexperienced pastor sitting in front of her wasn't going to ignore her counsel.

It was mid-winter of my first year in ordained ministry. Twelve months earlier I had been a third year seminary student, anticipating the likelihood of a call to a parish somewhere in the lower forty-eight states, but not knowing where. Now, here I was as the young, totally inexperienced pastor of a wonderful congregation in Kansas farmland. Graciously sitting with me in my study was that congregation's beloved organist and choir director. Sybil was a joy to work with, as the previous six months had proven. Rarely, however, had she advanced any strong recommendations to me about forthcoming worship services. Instead, she regularly had received my suggestions about hymns and such and forged ahead with keyboard accompaniment of the congregation's weekly voicing of those same hymns of my choice.

Now, here in my study the two of us were planning for the services of the approaching, springtime season of Lent. And lo and behold Sybil had quietly but emphatically objected to my brainstormed recommendations of hymns she could play during the approaching Maundy Thursday service's time of remembering Jesus's instituting of what we call the Lord's Supper. "It's not that I don't like the hymns you're suggesting, Pastor Bob. But in this instance each year, when Maundy Thursday comes, my experience has been that silence during the distribution of the Bread and the Cup has proven to be very meaningful." That was about the extent of her explanation, as best I can recall. But it was how she made her appeal—with conviction and grace—that made the difference to me.

"So, your suggestion is that once I've read through the liturgy for Communion, and the elders come forward to take the trays of bread and juice down the aisles, that all of that be done in absolute silence?"

"Yes, Pastor Bob, that *is* what I suggest."

A couple of months later, Holy Week arrived. On Palm Sunday hymns about Jesus's entry into Jerusalem had been sung with gusto. The service was replete with anthems and songs galore. And fittingly so, I sensed.

Four days later, the same congregation gathered in the same sanctuary. But all present displayed an entirely different demeanor. The earlier, loud "hosannas" were now almost a distant memory. Opening the worship hour, we sang a couple of somber hymns about Jesus's quiet, determined attitude of preparation for what lay ahead: a farcical trial, a mob's insistence he die in place of Barabbas, a gruesome flogging, and ultimately a horrific death by crucifixion. But when it came time for all in the sanctuary to share in the reenactment of the Last Supper, Sybil's counsel bore undeniable fruit. While the elders passed the trays of little cubes of bread and of small cups of grape juice, not one word was spoken. Nor sung.

The silence was heavy. And it was astonishingly fitting for the moment. As I watched from my seat behind the Communion Table, I beheld a collection of six dozen adults and youth receive the elements and then let the meaning of those elements take root. The absolute quiet of the setting was stirring for each and all. Including for me, who had never before experienced intentional silence in worship while pondering that upper room scene two millennia ago.

Sybil's advice was illuminating for me. Inclined to be more loquacious than pensive, I confess I had allowed my reliance on words—including those sung in hymns and anthems—to define the worship services I had begun to lead over the previous half year since my ordination. While that reliance may have proved appropriate in some worship settings, it wouldn't have that first Maundy Thursday in my young ministry. Sybil knew it.

Now I began to recognize it, as well.

In fact, in the four decades since that Maundy Thursday service, I've found myself again and again recalling the potency of silence in any number of settings. Those settings have included a variety of worship gatherings, including memorial services, Christmas Eve midnight watch hours, and even youth group camping retreats on quiet lakeshores. Those settings have also included demanding committee meetings and congregational budget deliberations. And maybe most importantly, those settings have included countless moments of pastoral engagement: in my study with troubled individuals and couples, in hospital rooms with the sick and dying, and in living rooms with bereaved family members planning their beloved ones' funeral services.

Silence in so many instances—and in so many contexts—has allowed for a listening to the one who most deeply listens to us, and who most restoratively speaks to us, as well.

How grateful I remain still for Sybil's quiet insistence no keyboard would be played, no voices raised, no words uttered while the family of God remembered the one sent into the midst of broken humanity in order to redeem that same humanity by himself being broken.

Words do no justice. Only silence does. Only silence.

17

Keepers

From mid-May through mid-November, virtually every Sunday noon I found myself remembering Gerry and Betty. Each time, I confess, I would shake my head in sadness, wondering how I, along with the wider community, could have been there in more sustaining ways for them, our brother and sister.

Gerry and Betty had long been members of the congregation in Kansas I served as pastor in the early 1980s. Together they farmed in the northwest corner of Lincoln County. They raised a small number of dairy cattle, as well as some egg producing chickens. But like most of their farming neighbors in the county, their primary agricultural focus was growing winter wheat.

Early on in my ministry with their congregation, I began to learn a bit about wheat farming. Gerry, in his patient way, explained to me how winter wheat was sown in the autumn, allowing for early growth of the plant stalk prior to the arrival of the harsh, windblown months of winter. The farmers' hope would be for some good, deep snowfall in the first few weeks of winter. That snow pack would provide a protective blanket for the foot tall stalks, as well as the blessing of nourishing watering of the plants as the cold began to wane. Once the snow pack had fully melted away by early to mid spring, those millions upon millions of wheat stalks would begin their remarkable growth into the several feet tall acreage that give wheat fields their unmistakable, gorgeous look of a tan colored sea. In due course, as spring fully yielded to the heat of summer, that winter wheat would move towards its full maturity. In that part of northern Kansas, the maturing process meant harvest typically arrived by late August or early September.

In early August, just one year after my wife and I had moved to the county, Gerry and Betty invited me out to their farm for a "look-see," as they called it. The wheat fields were stunning to behold. A light breeze, accompanying a cloudless, sunny sky, gave their expansive wheat fields a look of incomparable glory. What was particularly memorable was hearing Gerry say in his understated way, "Look what God has done." Not "what we have done," but God. I distinctly recall thinking to myself, "I need to get Gerry in the pulpit someday. His faith is compelling."

But then the storm came. And everything changed for Gerry and Betty. Everything.

Heading to bed on a Thursday night, I did as I was learning to do in that farming community. I tuned our radio to the local weather forecast. The prediction was for some significant rainfall, which sounded encouraging, given how little precipitation that part of the state had received in the past several weeks. One last watering of the mature wheat fields would have the crop in wonderful shape for the fast approaching harvest.

But Friday morning dawned, and with it news on that local radio station that a weather anomaly had unfolded between 2:00 and 4:00 a.m. Shaving in our little bathroom, I listened as the weather reporter—easily the most important individual on the airwaves in Kansas—noted soberly that a storm had indeed coursed its way through the counties to the west, and had then moved into Lincoln County. But the weatherman then reported that the storm had inexplicably stalled. Sounding as somber as I had ever yet heard the reporter, he explained, "For whatever reason, the system stopped for two full hours right over the northwest quarter of Lincoln County, and then dumped up to four inches of rain." After a moment of jolting quiet, he continued. "Early reports from farmers in those parts are that the wheat fields have been flattened. The loss looks to be total."

"What?" I mumbled to myself, staring blankly in the mirror. "Flattened wheat fields? Total loss?" A shiver of confusion—and then of fear—coursed through me. Then, recalling what part of the county I had visited just a handful of days earlier, I said aloud, "Oh no. Gerry and Betty." I dropped my razor straight into the sink, did a quick rinse of my still stubbly face, made quick use of my towel, and headed straight to the kitchen phone.

Shaking so much I had difficulty dialing their number, I called. Betty answered quietly, "Hello?"

"Betty, it's Pastor Bob."

Before I was able to say another word, Betty said quietly, "Gerry's out in the fields. He can't talk now." Then, with a sob, "It's all gone."

"Oh no, Betty," was all I managed to say at first. Then I asked, "May I come out?"

In a shockingly gracious manner, given their horrific circumstances, she responded, "Please. I think we'll both need to talk."

Less than half an hour later I turned left off the county road that headed north towards the Nebraska border. Within a handful of minutes, I began to see it. Heading due west, farm after farm, to my right and to my left, had indeed been impacted by the crushing rainfall of just a handful of hours earlier. Ironically, with the sky once again cloudless and the sun shining gloriously behind me in the east, everything around me looked wet. And pancake flat.

Acre after acre of fields no longer displayed glorious waves of wheat, begging to be harvested. Instead, those fields were a shocking landscape of muddied, squashed wheat stalks. Not one was standing upright. Every single one of the millions and millions of stalks were embedded in a damp blanket of dirt. All because the storm stalled—and then rained down havoc on the harvest-ready crop.

I very soon came to the driveway of the farm that had been given stewardly care for decades by Gerry and Betty, and by Gerry's parents and grandparents before them. By the time I parked in the driveway separating their home from their barn, it was nauseatingly evident the wheat was no more. That year's whole crop was destroyed.

There stood Gerry, evidently awaiting my arrival. I parked and began walking towards my dear friend. What quickly struck me was the understandable change in his demeanor since our previous visit. At that time he had declared in a soul warming way, "Look what God has done." Now his face suggested a sense of divine betrayal, rather than heavenly blessing. His eyes, red with sorrow, wordlessly cried out, "*Now* look what God has done."

For the next few minutes we walked slowly and talked softly. We took in the galling sight of their property, now looking far more like a woesome, sodden mudflat than a joyous field of dreams. We ended up sitting in their kitchen with Betty. There the three of us then tried to make sense of the senseless, and to think aloud of the implications thereof. With Betty holding her dear husband's hand, she said aloud the unspeakable. "This is it, isn't it, Gerry?"

He nodded, with tears streaming down his face. "It's over, yes." Turning to me, he explained. "We put all our reserves into this crop. Everything. Our yields the past few years were adequate to keep us afloat, but barely." He choked, and then said, "But we didn't have enough left over to buy much crop insurance. What little coverage we have won't come close to matching our losses of last night. The bank will foreclose, probably by the end of December. They'll possibly let us keep this house, but the land will be seized."

Betraying my naiveté, I asked quietly, "What will become of the land?"

Betty answered, seeing Gerry's lips quiver. "It'll be bought up by one of a handful of large corporations who've begun nationwide to grab any and all small family farms that aren't able to compete with them." Then glancing at her husband, she added, "The day of small family farmers, like us, is dying. All it takes is one disaster like last night . . ." No more words were spoken.

Within the next several months, the bank did its thing. Foreclosure on the land ensued. Gerry and Betty remained in their home, but Gerry did what neither he, nor his parents nor grandparents had ever done: took a line job in the county's one factory that manufactured widgets of one kind or another. He did so in abject misery. By the following summer, Gerry informed me that he and Betty had decided it was time for them to move. Uprooting themselves from the only home they had ever known, they moved two hundred miles west, where Gerry was hired by a massive cattle feeding company. My last communication with them suggested they were each experiencing wrenching despondency.

Two summers after that devastating, two hour long rainfall, I learned the following. A large agricultural conglomerate—based many hundreds of miles away from Lincoln County—had not only purchased their farm land from the bank. It had hired, at low wages, a handful of county residents who were desperate for work. Those employees oversaw the sowing of a new crop of winter wheat, and ultimately helped in its late summer harvest—a harvest that netted the conglomerate fabulous profits. And where did those profits go? Not to any residents, much less family farmers, in Lincoln County. They went to the conglomerate's thousands of shareholders, many of whom in all likelihood have never seen a glorious wheat field up close.

A quarter of a century then passed by.

Now the pastor of a wonderful congregation in upstate New York, I received a phone call on an ordinary Wednesday morning in early February. "Pastor Luidens?" asked a male voice that had a mild Dutch accent. "My name is Jan." When I greeted him in return, he continued. "My wife Beatrix and I are farmers. We have a small farm about eight miles west of your church's village. And we run a CSA from our farm."

When he stopped, I responded. "A CSA? I don't think I know what that is."

"Oh," he said, "a CSA is a Community Supported Agriculture. It's a program that connects small, family farms with surrounding communities who help ensure those farms survive." Before I had the chance to comment, he asked, "May I come by to discuss our CSA and your congregation? I think you'll find it of interest."

Having virtually no idea what such a conversation would entail, I nonetheless responded, "If that would be helpful to you, of course." We then scheduled a visit.

A week later Jan walked into my study at the church. An hour later he departed. In a state of wonderment, I then proceeded to draft a proposal for consideration by our congregation's governing board at its approaching monthly meeting.

The proposal recommended that our congregation become the rent-free site for the CSA's weekly distribution of freshly harvested items from Jan and Beatrix's modest family farm. Per the basic model of all CSAs, Jan and Beatrix would invite members of our local community to purchase "shares" in that year's harvested produce from their farm. One share might cost four hundred dollars for the entire year. If one hundred families each purchased such a share, they would each then be entitled to one hundredth of each week's harvest. Jan and Beatrix's farm included everything from tomatoes and cucumbers, to scallions and pumpkins. Each Friday morning they would harvest whatever produce was ready that week, would then truck it from their farm to our church building, and make it available in our fellowship hall to all one hundred shareholders to pick up that afternoon and evening.

And the relationship between Jan and Beatrix's CSA and the congregation? It was quite simple. The CSA had in the church's fellowship hall a free distribution site that was easily accessible to everyone in our village who bought a share in the CSA. In turn, each week the congregation was allowed to keep whatever produce was left over by the end of that Friday's distribution. In any given week a significant portion of the produce would not be picked up by the shareholders, be it because they might not want leeks or kale, or because they were traveling on vacation. We, the congregation, would then retain those food items from Friday evening, and would make them freely available in that same fellowship hall for any interested worshippers two days later, on Sunday noon after worship.

The church's governing board reviewed the above proposal, affirmed it, and our relationship with the CSA commenced. And it thrived.

The governing board decided to invite free will contributions from any Sunday worshippers who took home some of the leftovers, such as ears of corn, bags of turnips, or a fresh pumpkin. Those contributions ultimately added up by the time Thanksgiving arrived. What came of those cash contributions? The congregation forwarded it all, every last penny, to the village's food pantry that was housed in the nearby Catholic Church's fellowship hall. That food pantry's volunteers then used that sum of several hundred dollars to purchase fresh produce during the ensuing winter months—fresh produce for those who otherwise might not be able to afford it at the local supermarket.

This relationship between Jan and Beatrix's CSA and the congregation took hold. It has remained in place for years. The benefits? All village residents who have bought shares in the CSA have enjoyed wonderful, locally grown produce. Additionally, members of the congregation have feasted on leftover items, week after week. All who have gone to the food pantry in the dead of winter have received fresh vegetables and fruit. And Jan and Beatrix? They have been able to afford to remain in the incomparable vocation of local, family farming. Because if and when a two hour rain storm might one summer's night cause the utter devastation of their farm's produce, they won't have their farm foreclosed by a bank. Why? Because the shares purchased by the one hundred local families will sustain them throughout. The shareholders share the farmers' risk, enabling the family farm to survive, no matter the circumstances from year to year.

Which brings me back to Gerry and Betty.

Once my congregation in New York had been given this priceless gift of partnering with Jan and Beatrix's CSA, I found myself harkening back, with a pained heart, to what had befallen Gerry and Betty so many years earlier back in Kansas. From mid-May through mid-November, virtually every Sunday noon I now found myself remembering the life crushing moment two and a half decades earlier when their family farm had fallen victim to the rain—and to the travesty of an economic system that allowed their financial wellbeing to implode with nothing—and no one—to sustain them. Absent any who "shared" in their vulnerability, they—and their family farm—were robbed of the vitality every family farm is meant to embody.

Each of those Sunday noontimes, I confess, I would shake my head in sadness. Week after week I found myself wondering how, in more sustaining ways, the wider community of Lincoln County could have been there for Gerry and Betty.

I don't know the answer to that felt conundrum. It may be that our world's economic systems are so complex, if not compromised, that much of the blessed vocation of family farming is, for all practical purposes, destined to die. But if and when we, God's children, can learn to walk alongside of the vulnerable—be they family farmers or any others who are easily abused by the forces of our broken world's economic orders—we are called to do so. We are called to be shareholders with the vulnerable.

Early in the narratives embodied in the first book of the Jewish and Christian scriptures, Eve and Adam's son Cain asked of his Lord a question that strikes me as germane to all of the above. Having just witnessed Cain's horrific act of fratricide, God demands of Cain, "Where is your brother

Abel?" Cain's impudent question in response? "Am I my brother's keeper?" (Genesis 4:9) God did not respond with, "Of course you are!" But the moment insisted that our maker felt—and feels—just that. We are to be those who care for one another, especially in our places and vocations of vulnerability. We are indeed to be our sisters' and brothers' keepers.

No calling is more essential. No service is more fulfilling.

18

Miriam's Shoes

Miriam and I sat opposite each other in my study. The silence was almost excruciating. While I looked Miriam in the eye, as compassionately as possible, she understandably looked downward—not so much at her shoes as at her life.

The year was 1984, a decade after the landmark decision of the U.S. Supreme Court now known as Roe v. Wade. It was in the aftermath of that legal ruling about a woman's constitutional right to have an abortion that now had Miriam sitting stone still some ten feet in front of me. She was pondering how to respond. I had just asked her, as gently as possible, "How do *you* feel about Jimmy's suggestion?"

I had, for all practical purposes, no idea whatsoever what her response might be to that hard but essential question.

Miriam and I had come to be good friends over the previous two years. She was a member of the congregation I was serving in our wonderful Kansas farming town. Unlike most of the members of the congregation who had been born and raised in the county, she had grown up in Denver, some four hundred miles to the west. A gifted administrator, with a master's degree in agricultural law, she had been hired by a legal firm to work in support of the local wheat and cattle farmers. As I had learned from many of the farming families, she was highly regarded. Jimmy was part of one of those families, a college graduate who was now working on his parents' farm, expected to take over for them once they retired in the years ahead.

Four months before our quiet meeting in my study, Miriam had brought her fiancé Jimmy to meet with me for the purpose of scheduling their wedding the following summer. I found myself delighted by their company and happy for both of them. We began to meet monthly to do some traditional pre-marital counseling, and I was deeply impressed by their self-awareness and honest transparency with each other and with me.

But then came the day of the quiet conversation with Miriam alone. She phoned on a Monday morning, sobbing while asking to see me. Within ten minutes she was sitting in my study, not looking me in the eye as she typically did. Now she was staring at her shoes, tears running down her face.

For the better part of the first minute she was silent. "What is it, Miriam?" I asked her as gently as possible.

She looked up at me, then back down again. "It's Jimmy." But then, "No, it's actually me. Or both of us." She shook her head, wiped her now wet cheeks with her hand, and said, "Jimmy wants me to get an abortion." I recall her choking on the last word. She began to sob.

I stood and brought to her the box of tissues sitting on my desk. She grabbed three or four, wiping some of her tears away. But she continued to sob.

I sat quietly, waiting for her to let me know if and when she was ready to talk. After a full minute, which felt like an hour, she shook her head, both sadly and angrily. "This is so hard to talk about, Pastor Bob." I nodded silently. "But I need to think this through, and there's no one else in town I can talk about this with." I nodded again. "I guess I'd better explain."

"Share whatever you feel would be helpful, Miriam," I said, realizing I was on pastorally uncharted territory. To this point in my life, I had never once discussed abortion with anyone other than in academic settings.

"Well, a couple of months ago Jimmy and I got more physical than usual." She stopped. I waited. She continued. "We thought that he was protected. I let him put the condom on himself, and he told me he was sure it was on all the way." She stopped again. I waited. "When we were done we realized it hadn't stayed on all the way." After some angry silence, she said, "I was furious with him! And I was furious with myself, letting him be the one to be in charge of this." I waited, and then she said with a glance sideways and a hunching of her shoulders, "And of course I then missed my period, got a testing kit, and here I am." She stopped again. "I'm pregnant."

I nodded, choosing again not to interrupt.

She then said sadly, "When I told him yesterday that I was pregnant, he just shrugged. He just *shrugged*, Pastor Bob, and then he said, 'Well, just drive down to Wichita and have it taken care of. That's where they do it.'" Silence. Then she said with intensity, "He had clearly been thinking all along about the possibility I would be pregnant, but he had decided all on his own that I should get an abortion. We hadn't talked at all for the last six weeks about the possibility I was pregnant. But yesterday I tell him I'm carrying our child, and he's already made up his mind." She stopped, and then shook her head back and forth, betraying grief, confusion, and ire.

I nodded and remained silent. When it was clear Miriam had shared with me as much as she was ready to for the moment, I said as gently as possible, "I'm sorry, Miriam. I can't imagine your pain right now." She nodded, seeming to accept my effort at sympathy. Additional silence followed. Uncertain if it were even a fair question to pose at this particular moment, I asked, "How do *you* feel about Jimmy's suggestion?"

Miriam continued to look downward. Definitely not at me. Then slowly she looked up and said, "I honestly don't know what I feel. And I definitely don't know what to do." I nodded and waited. "If I choose to abort, it feels like the problem will go away. No embarrassment for me. No shockwaves for Jimmy." Silence. "But if I choose to carry the baby to term, I doubt I'll be allowed to keep my job here. I could easily get fired, and you know as well as anyone no one around here will ever hire me again. I'll have to go back to Denver, have the baby there, and then try to start all over, on my own. Jimmy won't be able to leave the farm. We'll be through, and I'll be a single mother." She stopped, tearing up once again. "I don't know what to do, Pastor Bob." I nodded, acknowledging the profound complexity of her circumstance: while Jimmy had easily suggested abortion as the obvious choice, Miriam was the one—truly the only one—who had to live, in full, with the decision.

I've thought about our conversation countless times over the four decades since that Monday morning. What she bravely shared with me has come to mind frequently when I've happened upon the endless debates about Roe v. Wade. While I'm convinced that the many and varied factors in those debates are worthy of consideration—theological, constitutional, societal, economic—the real-life concerns of those such as Miriam, in my estimation, must always be the ultimate frame for those debates. I confess until and unless one is in Miriam's shoes, no one else is fit to presume to walk in them for her.

Miriam went to Wichita five days later. Jimmy drove.

I visited with Miriam two weeks thereafter. Once again she came to my study. As before, she sat much of the time staring sadly at her feet. I invited her to tell me whatever she felt led to share. To my surprise she described in great detail what that long day of sorrow in Wichita entailed. She described the sense of desolation. Even of isolation. She noted that Jimmy was quiet most of the ride to and from Wichita, clearly relieved, but also matching in an unquantifiable way some of the deep grief Miriam was feeling. When I asked, she noted her own sense of fracture. She said unflinchingly her life would never be the same. "Do I feel I made the right decision, Pastor Bob?"

she posed. "I don't know. I don't know if I'll ever know." After a pause, she added, "I don't know if there *is* a right decision."

We talked quietly for the better part of two hours. There was no moment when we came to a place of any resolution, whatever that might mean. But we affirmed that as her life unfolded, our God would always hold her and Jimmy—and every precious soul—in gracious embrace.

Several months later Miriam and Jimmy stood before me and the assembly of their loved ones and friends, exchanging marriage vows. I moved from Kansas to upstate New York soon thereafter, losing contact with them in due course. I trust, though, that our consoling creator yet looks upon Miriam with a calming grace and an understanding heart no one else can come close to matching.

19

Bar-Jonah

The Old Testament is replete with odd characters. But few of them are more puzzling, if not disturbing, than Jonah.

Going all the way back to my youth, Sunday school teachers who introduced Jonah's story never failed to draw from within me both childlike curiosity and juvenile nausea. Listening to the teachers' accounts, I was always intrigued by Jonah's pugnacious insistence on sailing away westward to Tarshish, rather than trudging off eastward to Nineveh, as divinely directed. I then inevitably found my innards repulsed by his being gobbled up—though, oddly enough, not digested—by the proverbial whale. That same sea serpent then disgorged Jonah, apparently intact, back onto land. From then and there his ordained trek to Nineveh awaited.

Little did I know that a quarter of a century after those early Sunday school lessons I would find myself relating to that same Jonah.

It was late spring of 1984. My wife Mary and I, along with our infant firstborn, were thick in the process of investigating where it might be that we were meant to move. Now approaching the close of our three-year commitment to serve our treasured patients and parishioners in Kansas, we were facing a major decision. After extensive communication, travel, and interviews earlier that spring, my wife and I found ourselves having to decide. Would we be moving to northern New Jersey or to upstate New York? Both options were enticing.

A fascinating congregation in New Jersey had extended the promise of a call, were I to accept it. Their property was near a main highway that funneled countless thousands of commuters into New York City on a daily basis. Were we to move to that parish, my wife would then join those commuters in order to continue her specialized training at a prestigious medical center in Manhattan.

The alternative move would take us to a village in upstate New York, on the outskirts of Albany one hundred and fifty miles to the north of Manhattan. In that delightful community another congregation's search committee had informed me I was one of two final candidates for their pastoral position. A thirty-minute drive from their parsonage was an esteemed medical center in downtown Albany, where Mary could pursue her desired training.

Back in Kansas, with the above options staring us in the vocational face, we deliberated. We prayerfully weighed our options. We found ourselves drawn one day to one choice, and the next to the other. It began to wear on us

Then came the Jonah event.

It was Sunday afternoon. With that morning's worship responsibilities in the rear view mirror, Mary and I talked about our immediate future. As we did so, I felt mounting pressure. The next evening at seven p.m. the search committee of the church in upstate New York was scheduled to meet. That committee's chair, Charles, had informed me the committee was planning on engaging in the process of prayerful discernment: which of their two final candidates would they feel led to recommend to the church's governing board to be called as the congregation's next pastor? Would it be I, or the other?

By late evening that Sunday back in Kansas, it happened. Sensing God was directing us to move to New Jersey, rather than to upstate New York, Mary and I agreed it would behoove me to let Charles and his committee know prior to Monday evening that they should remove my name from their list of two potential candidates. Better, I thought to myself, that they then could recommend the other candidate as their first choice, than potentially to recommend me, only thereafter to be compelled to recommend their second choice were I to pull out of the process after the decisive meeting. Having made that prayerful decision on Sunday evening, Mary and I agreed I would call Charles from my church study early Monday morning.

Eight a.m. arrived. I dialed Charles's home phone. His wife answered. She noted her husband was already at work. She gave me his office number, which I dialed. When he answered, I began, with no small measure of emotion, "Good morning, Charles. This is Bob, calling from Kansas." Not surprisingly, he responded with his warm, understated grace. After a brief reference to the church in New Jersey, I said, "I'm calling to let you and the search committee know that my wife and I have given much prayer to what lies ahead and where it is God is calling us to move. We now believe we are meant to move to New Jersey, not upstate New York."

Again not surprisingly, Charles responded, "Well, that's disappointing to hear. I was looking forward to the committee's deliberations this evening, with the real possibility they would feel led to recommend your name to the governing board."

"I'm humbled to hear you say that, Charles," I responded. "In truth, Mary and I decided last night that I should call you this morning with our decision so as to save the committee from what could be a frustrating, if not counterproductive, meeting."

"That was good of you, Bob," Charles said. "Please tell Mary 'Thank you' for me."

As I responded, "You're very welcome, Charles," I realized my words did not slide out easily. My voice seemed to miss a beat. As did my heart.

After a minute or two more of sincerely warm words exchanged between the two of us, I hung up. Then I sat in absolute stillness at my desk. Where typically I would then have reached for my Monday "to do" list, made the previous Friday afternoon, I failed to do so. Instead, I sat stock still.

In the silence that followed, I became aware of something to that point in my life never yet experienced. My soul began to ache. Or more truthfully, it began to feel a pain unlike anything I had previously known. My whole chest began to tighten, and then to feel as if on fire.

Words still fail me, other than to say I felt the absolute absence of peace. It felt like I had fallen headlong into an abyss.

And then: "Oh no." I heard myself say aloud, "We're supposed to move to upstate New York. Not New Jersey." As soon as I said those words, I began to moan. Were anyone else to have been in the church building at that moment, they would have come running, understandably concerned I might be having a heart attack or worse. "What have I done?" erupted from my lips.

It was my Jonah moment. "Not to Tarshish, Bob. To Nineveh."

I honestly have little memory of what I did for the next hour or two. Desperate for someone to walk alongside me through this soul-thrashing moment, I ultimately did what I rarely if ever had done. I stumbled out the church door, climbed into my car, and drove to the nearby medical clinic where Mary was embroiled in her care of a steady stream of outpatients. I parked and entered through the back door. Janice, the front desk staff person, quick to recognize the look of peril on my face, jumped up from her seat and said, "I'll get Dr. Mary right away."

Thirty seconds later Janice pulled me into an empty examining room, sat me down, looked me in the eye, and announced, "She'll be here momentarily."

As predicted, Mary joined me in the quiet room. "Are you okay?" she asked both gently and seriously.

I could barely find my voice. "No," I managed to say. "I'm a mess."

"How so?" she asked, now sitting down right in front of me, reaching out to take one of my shaking hands.

"I think—no, I know—I've made a huge mistake." Blinking back tears, I continued. "I called Charles this morning. To tell him about our decision last night." Mary nodded her understanding. "I told him we'd decided to move to New Jersey, and to take my name off their list for tonight's meeting." She nodded again. "But as soon as I hung up—" I stopped, unable to find the words.

"As soon as you hung up, what?" Mary asked softly.

"I felt unbelievable pain. I can't even describe it. My chest hurt. My whole body broke into a cold sweat. I could barely breathe." Mary nodded, but remained silent. "And it hit me: we were supposed to move to upstate New York, not to New Jersey."

Mary looked me in the eye. She remained silent for a stretch. Maybe it was five seconds. Maybe five minutes. I honestly don't recall. But then, while I sat there in utter desolation, she spoke directly and with astonishing, quiet conviction. "Well, then we should move to upstate New York."

I stared in disbelief at her. "It's too late! I told Charles to take my name off their little list."

Nodding her understanding, Mary then said, "Well, call him up again. Tell him what you're now feeling, asking him to keep your name on their list for tonight's meeting." The direct, unambiguous way she gave me her counsel was astonishing.

"Call him up and tell him to put my name back on?" I responded, with a tone of disbelief. I confess, even four decades later, I thought Mary had lost any semblance of rationality. "If I do that, what's he going to say? What's the committee going to say? 'Oh, Bob's just the kind of pastor we want: someone who changes his mind about where to work from one minute to the next. Yeah, let's call that guy to be our spiritual leader.' They'll laugh their heads off tonight if Charles tells them."

To which my amazing wife responded, "Well, think about it. If they respond that way, they won't recommend you, and they and you will never see each other again." And then she said quietly, "But just the opposite may happen. They may hear about your experience today, and may take that as indication God is saying to you, 'Bob, you're to go to upstate New York. Not New Jersey.' In which case, they may well say, 'If that's God's plan, let's be part of it.'"

Still to this day, I recall thinking, "My word, she's right."

After then sharing as warm a hug together as we'd ever yet had in the first seven years of our marriage, my wife returned to her ministry of medical care, and I drove back to the church. I dialed Charles's phone at work. No answer. I called his home. None there either. For the next seven hours I tried again and again to reach him, but to no avail.

Finally, a handful of minutes before the seven p.m. opening prayer of the search committee's decisive meeting at the church in New York, I got through to Charles at the church. When he answered my umpteenth attempt to reach him, we had a brief but transformative exchange. I explained, in short but succinct detail, what I had experienced following our morning phone conversation. I then said, "Charles, I know what I'm going to ask of you and the committee is out of the ordinary, if not inexplicable. But I would ask that you let everyone know I would welcome their putting my name back on your short list."

To my utter astonishment Charles responded, "I'll gladly do so." Then he said, "I arrived about ten minutes ago, along with several other early birds. When I told them about your call this morning, they were uniformly disappointed. When I tell them now what you've been through today, and that you are open to having your name put back on the list, I'm guessing they'll all be delighted."

I could barely believe my ears. Maybe because I had failed to believe my Lord.

"Thank you, Charles," I managed to say. We hung up.

Two hours later our phone in Kansas rang. It was Charles. "Bob, I'm calling to let you know the committee has enthusiastically voted to recommend your name to the governing board. We truly believe you're meant to be our next pastor." Our exchange was surprisingly brief, but profoundly inspiring.

That summer the three of us moved from Kansas to upstate New York. We remained there for more than thirty-one years. Mary and I raised our three beloved children as part of that congregation and community. In fact, Mary and I remained there until we retired.

It may be a scriptural stretch to suggest my experience of that Monday in the spring of 1984 somehow parallels Jonah's story. But as the years have passed, I've often allowed myself to recall the spirit-wrenching time at my desk after my morning call to Charles. I've wondered whether Jonah may have endured just such a calamity while gripping the side of the storm-tossed ship headed toward Tarshish. Jonah's God ultimately led his boat-mates to toss him overboard, straight into the whale's mouth, and ultimately back onto the shore that led to Nineveh. Likewise, my God ultimately said,

"No. Turn around. Go where I am calling you to go. Not to Tarshish. To Nineveh."

Do I understand the mystery embedded in Jonah's story? Do I understand the one embedded in my own?

All these years later I confess I will never understand such mysteries. But I will never, ever deny them. Rather, I welcome them. They give meaning to life in ways that are beyond measure.

20

Table for All

BEING USHERED TO THE front of the gathering space was unexpected in its own right. But what ultimately unfolded while sitting in that front row was beyond any measure of predictability—or grace.

It was early autumn. My wife and I, along with our infant daughter, had recently moved from Kansas to upstate New York. I had begun to settle into my second parish as pastor of a wonderful Reformed congregation in the village. Part of the settling in had included beginning to forge what would become deeply supportive and inspirational friendships with the pastors of the two other congregations in the village—Keen, a Lutheran minister, and Bob, a Roman Catholic priest.

While I was relatively new to the ordained ministry, Keen and Bob were well into several decades of vocational service with parishes in their respective denominations. I began to get to know them during our weekly, two hour long, Tuesday morning coffee visits in the Catholic rectory's comfortable living room. While I had enjoyed a small handful of fledgling friendships with some counterpart pastors in my first, short ministry in Kansas, none of those friendships prefigured the kind of spiritual resonance I would ultimately come to treasure with Keen and Bob. By the third or fourth week together as a threesome, I realized I was in the company of exceptional mentors.

Their mentoring came in the form of gentle—and incisive—reflection together about various dynamics we confronted in our pastoral responsibilities. It was apparent early on that each was deeply involved in the lives of their many church members. As committed as both of them were to excellence as worship leaders, they were all the more dedicated to faithful engagement with all of their parishioners. Daily they were on the road to hospitals, nursing homes, and even prisons, embodying Christ's faithful presence in all circumstances.

Father Bob, as many of his Catholic parishioners called their beloved priest, was living testimony to the powerful witness of someone who had no inclination to be self-promoting. As prominent a member of the village community that Bob was, he yet modeled humility as few others have in my experience. By way of example, it was Keen who had to tell me what Bob on his own never would about the day he declined the august honor of a Papal audience. Five years prior to my meeting Keen and Bob, Pope John Paul II had traveled from Rome to the United States, visiting several cities nationwide, at each location leading worship in large venues. One such setting was in a stadium in Philadelphia. Bob's presiding Bishop in upstate New York invited Bob to be the one priest from their entire diocese chosen to travel to Philadelphia in order to concelebrate the Mass alongside the Holy Father—an honor, I suspect, most Catholic priests would have been ecstatic to accept. But not Bob. In Bob's quiet presence, Keen described to me how Bob had responded to his Bishop, "Thanks, but I have important work to do here in my parish." Such was Father Bob's commitment to his vocation—and to his beloved parishioners.

It was that Father Bob who ushered me to the front of the gathering space.

Five days earlier an esteemed villager had passed away. Dr. Grover had been long time physician to thousands of residents in and around our county, as well as faithful member of the village's Catholic parish. It became quickly apparent to me his death was a huge loss to all. Brand new to the community, I had not had the opportunity to meet and get to know him. Nonetheless, I decided to attend his funeral Mass and share in the celebration of his life with those who mourned his loss.

Because of the large numbers anticipated to be in attendance at the funeral, Father Bob arranged for the use of the Catholic church's large parish hall, rather than the somewhat smaller sanctuary, ensuring adequate space for all to sit. I arrived some twenty minutes prior to the start of the service, planning to take an inconspicuous seat in the far back corner. But Bob was at the door, welcoming everyone as they entered. Upon seeing me, he smiled, gave me his unparalleled hug, and then pulled me by my elbow straight up to the front of the hall. As he did so, he quietly whispered, "You'll sit right up here next to Keen." Sure enough, there was Keen, the Lutheran pastor, already sitting in close proximity to a host of empty chairs clearly reserved for Dr. Grover's kin. As Bob took me to the vacant seat next to Keen, he added firmly, "And you'll be receiving the elements." Before I had a chance to respond, he ensured I was in my chair. He then headed back to the entryway in order to welcome the large flow of still arriving guests.

I confess I was dumbfounded. Before I knew what to do, Keen squeezed my knee and whispered, "I'm glad you're here. It will mean the world to Dr. Grover's family."

Glancing around me, I was moved beyond words to behold countless folks in nearby chairs, looking right at me—smiling and nodding, as if to say, "You're right where you're meant to be." Such unspoken but undeniable graciousness touched me in immeasurable ways.

Several minutes later, funeral directors rolled the casket to the front of the hall, and then ushered in Dr. Grover's large extended family, all of whom sat to the left and right of Keen and me. Father Bob then moved to the lectern and warmly welcomed everyone to this time of worship.

For the next half hour or more, the liturgy unfolded, with appropriate thanks offered for the gift of Dr. Grover. Then the moment of unanticipated grace unfolded.

Father Bob moved to the Lord's Table and initiated the liturgical preparation for the sacrament of Holy Communion. While in earlier years I had attended a small handful of Roman Catholic services that included the sacrament, I had not partaken of the elements on any of those occasions. I understood the sacrament to be solely for those who are confessing Catholics. That being the case, I was still trying to take in the shock—and significance—of Bob's earlier whisper to me that I would be "receiving the elements." Could a Protestant pastor be offered—and receive—the holy elements of the Roman Catholic sacrament?

Before I had time to sort out the answer to that puzzling question, here came Father Bob, elements in hand, offering them first to Keen and me, and only then to Dr. Grover's family, and finally to the entire gathered congregation. What was astonishing to me was the simple fact Bob invited everyone present to receive the elements. No restriction about membership in the Catholic church was spoken. To the contrary, a welcome was implied—to any and all who would receive.

As best I could tell, glancing over my shoulder, very few opted not to receive.

The moment was one of pure grace. Of heart-stirring gift. Of restored community.

The following Tuesday I joined Bob and Keen in the rectory living room for our weekly conversation. I asked Bob about his assertive ushering of me to the front of the hall, and his insistence I join Keen in receiving the elements with our Catholic sisters and brothers. In his guileless manner, Bob smiled and said, "What better opportunity to reveal the love our God has for the whole church?" He looked at Keen, and each nodded. "What the three of us were able to do at esteemed Dr. Grover's funeral was make it clear to the whole community that everyone belongs. No one is barred—not just from the sacrament, but from God's family."

That was it. Though Father Bob might have chosen in that moment to wax even more theological, he didn't. His actions had spoken louder than any words could. His priestly compassion had revealed what God's grace is all about.

21

Broken

I was both stunned and, I confess, appalled. I thought to myself, "He's gotta be kidding." But the next few minutes of conversation suggested my father wasn't kidding in the least.

Dad and I were sitting under a shady maple tree. We were talking in the back yard of the parsonage my wife and I, along with our two very young daughters, called home. The four of us had been living there for the better part of three years. The first year had proven to be replete with encouraging experiences for both of us, Mary in her ongoing training as a physician, and me in my pastoral work with the congregation who had issued my call to serve. But years two and three had unfolded with increasing challenges for me—challenges unlike anything I had thus far experienced in my first handful of years in ordained ministry.

Decades later, even putting in writing what those challenges entailed remains soul-wrenching for me.

On an ordinary Sunday some months into my second year of installed ministry with the congregation, Saul found me in my study. The worship hour had ended thirty minutes earlier, and I was hanging up my preaching robe in my study. As was typically the case at that Sunday noontime juncture, I was fairly spent from the week that symbolically had just ended for me. I was ready to walk home for Sunday lunch and rest with my family. But that's when Saul knocked on my door and walked into my study. Saul was a young father, maybe a handful of years my elder. He and his family were fairly regular in attendance. "Hi, Saul," I said.

"Bob," he nodded in reply. Then, while taking a seat on the couch, he added, "I'm here to tell you what you probably already know."

"Oh," I responded, taking a seat opposite the couch. "What's up?"

"Well, it's your preaching. And the way you are, really." He stopped, looking me straight in the eye, as if I would understand exactly what it was to which he was referring.

In fact I had no idea what he had in mind. None whatsoever. "My preaching?" I responded. "And the way I am?" I began to feel not just confusion, but no small measure of discomfort.

"Well, it's becoming clear to me and to many others in the congregation that you're not Spirit-filled. At least not as Spirit-filled as a pastor should be." He stopped again, with a facial expression that seemed to say, "You know exactly what I mean." Which I did not.

So I said, "I'm going to need you to explain what you mean in a little more detail, Saul."

He continued to look directly at me, with no glance to the side that would suggest any discomfort he might have been feeling. It was evident he was sitting there, absolutely resolute in his conviction. What he was telling me he was saying without a trace of hesitancy. "You're clearly not filled with the Holy Spirit, Bob." I opted not to respond, if for no other reason than no words came to mind. He continued. "If you were truly filled with the Spirit, I would know. So would the others in the congregation who feel the same way."

All these years later I wish I could say I perceived an element of compassion embedded in Saul's words of critique. But I can't. Instead, I still recall Saul's icy demeanor. Rather than feeling hot under the collar, I began to experience a numbing coldness, both within and without.

Trying not to respond with the same frigidity I was experiencing, I managed to say, "You and others believe I'm not filled with the Holy Spirit?" He nodded and remained silent, seemingly awaiting further response from me. Grasping for whatever I might helpfully say under these uncharted conditions, I then said, "Well, it sounds like we should schedule a time to discuss this at greater length than we have right now." I naively anticipated such a suggestion would be graciously received.

I was wrong.

"Not sure how any conversation about this would be of any help, Bob," responded Saul. "What is, is." Again he stopped. Then he announced, "So I guess I'll be going." With that, he rose and walked out.

I barely had time to rise from my own seat in order to follow him to the door of my study. "Thank you for coming by," I may have mumbled. If I added, "Let's stay in touch," I doubt he could have heard it.

That Sunday noontime exchange proved to be the first of at least three more such conversations over the next twelve to eighteen months. In succession, other members of the congregation—all men—approached me at different times to convey their doubtless assessment I was not Spirit-filled.

In those successive conversations I more readily pressed for an explanation. In each instance the response included reference to my never speaking in tongues during worship. My prayers and my sermons betrayed no glossolalic abilities. That is to say, in their commonly shared opinion I lacked the charismatic gifts requisite for pastoral leadership.

To that point in time I had not been particularly aware of the presence in the congregation of the small but very committed number of married couples who self-identified as charismatic Christians. The vast majority of members of the congregation did not so identify. But what I began to piece together was an illuminating picture of the congregation's recent history.

Some years earlier, during the closing couple of years of my pastoral predecessor's work with the congregation, his gifts in worship leadership had apparently attracted Christians in the surrounding community who were looking for a home in which they could practice their spiritual gifts, including speaking in tongues. Their welcome into the congregation was sincerely expressed by my predecessor, resulting in a fascinating—and likely disorienting—mix of worship inclinations in the wider congregation. While the vast majority, including many who had been part of the congregation for decades, were drawn to traditional, liturgical worship, this newer collection of young couples were desiring more charismatic worship. In time my predecessor reportedly made significant efforts to meld both worship styles from Sunday to Sunday.

But then he quite suddenly resigned.

Twenty months later I was installed as the congregation's next pastor. But for whatever fascinating—and ultimately unhelpful—reasons, no one within the congregation spoke to me of the previous few years' unfolding and unfinished process of congregational self-defining. No one informed me of the subsurface dynamic of a large traditionalist majority and a small charismatic minority, all quietly waiting to see what the new pastor would do on Sunday mornings. All silently waiting to discern what worship style I would embody from week to week.

A bit more than one year after my installation that subsurface tension started to erupt, beginning with that quietly tectonic exchange in my study with Saul. When it became increasingly clear my worship leadership was exasperatingly traditional to the charismatic minority, they understandably became discouraged. In their discouragement they resolved to do what their deep convictions insisted: inform the relatively new pastor I was not gifted for further leadership of this congregation.

Which is where my backyard conversation with my father—a pastor himself—then came into play.

Dad was visiting our little family for the weekend. He had attended that Sunday morning and then stayed for lunch with our family. Now sitting beneath the maple tree, the two of us had time for a quiet chat. Several minutes into our visit, in his inestimably gentle way Dad asked, "So, how are things in the congregation?"

Knowing my father, it was clear he was inviting full and honest disclosure. Which is what he got. "Well, Dad, it's become something of a struggle."

"How so?"

"It's challenging to describe, but here goes." I then detailed the several conversations I had had going all the way back to Saul's noontime visit in my study almost two years earlier. As best I could, I explained how I was making great efforts to listen carefully to those who had assessed me to be less than fully Spirit-filled, at the same time as remaining true to my own convictions about worship leadership. In a manner I presumed Dad would well appreciate, I detailed how I was committed to providing pastoral and worship leadership that would optimize the likelihood of congregational unity. My goal was to ensure each and every member of the congregation would feel at home, nourished by the Spirit who called us together in the first place.

When I had finally spelled out in detail what the previous couple of years had entailed for me, Dad quietly nodded his appreciation for my explanation. "Sounds like it's turned into a conundrum of sorts. Both for you as well as for the congregation, and especially for your charismatic members." I nodded, anticipating a subsequent "There, there, Bob. It'll be fine."

Was my anticipation ever misguided.

Rather than saying "There, there, Bob," my father said, "Well, have you suggested, or even told, the charismatics in your congregation where they might better go?" I stared at him, uncomprehending. "Is there a Christian congregation within driving distance of here where the worship service is fully charismatic?" He stopped, awaiting my response.

Still confounded by Dad's questions, I said, "Well, I know of at least one charismatic fellowship. It's maybe a twenty or thirty minute drive from here, according to one of the charismatic members in the congregation. He's told me he and his family go there for special renewal services from time to time."

"So there's at least one congregation in the area where the charismatic members of your congregation would likely feel more at home for worship?" Dad asked.

Now feeling increasingly ill at ease by Dad's questions, I nonetheless answered, "Yes, I guess so."

"Good. I'm glad to hear it." He then asked, "Have you informed them that that's where they should go? That they should move their membership from your congregation to a congregation that is known to be charismatic?"

I sat there under the maple tree, both stunned and, I confess, appalled. I still recall thinking to myself, "He's gotta be kidding." But the next few minutes of conversation suggested my father wasn't kidding in the least.

"No, Dad. I most certainly have not informed them of any such thing."

Before I gathered myself to say anything else, my father asked quietly, "Why not?"

It took me a few moments, but I managed to respond, "Because I don't believe that's what a pastor should do. I don't believe it's what my calling is about."

"How do you mean, Bob?"

"Dad," I said, now feeling both confusion and no small measure of anger, "I don't believe a pastor's job is to direct Christian brothers and sisters where they should worship. That's between themselves and God. If a charismatic member of my congregation believes he or she is called to be a member of my congregation, it's not for me to tell them, 'No, you should be a member of a different congregation.'" Dad continued to listen carefully, allowing me to forge on. "You apparently have a very different view. You think it's my duty or privilege or whatever to inform them they should attend elsewhere?"

Appearing to me to remain astonishingly unruffled, Dad responded with a quiet but nonetheless serious tone, "My experience, Bob, is that how each and every Christian worships is profoundly important. For any number of reasons, each of us finds that we are fed by a specific form of worship. For some of us—including you and me, it seems—a fairly traditional, liturgical style is most nourishing. For others of us, including the several families in your congregation who self-identify as charismatic, a more free, less liturgical style meets their needs—especially in the form of speaking in tongues." I nodded silently. "It seems to me one of your pastoral responsibilities is to help your Christian friends find the worship setting most fit for their spiritual needs." I nodded again. "In the case of the families who find your worship leadership less than enriching for them, they may need you to say, 'It's time for you to find your new congregational home. It's apparently not here in this congregation.'"

I realized my father was pulling me into unfamiliar waters as a young pastor. I responded, "But Dad, my sense of calling is rooted in a conviction that the church is one. That Christ's body is meant to be unified. I believe my ministry's goal is to foster, to model, that unity. I believe my calling is to enable traditional and charismatic Christians to be at one, not divided." I stopped, awaiting a response. His silence invited me to say more. "If I were to inform my charismatic members they should move their membership to another congregation, rather than to remain in fellowship with everyone else here, I feel as though I'd be betraying my calling."

Dad nodded. "I could see how that's how you might see it." Yet he then said, "But maybe it's not possible for you to mend the church on your own. Maybe it's not possible for you to be a pastor to a congregation that is deeply divided over worship style." He then said, "And maybe it's not up to the small minority of folks who desire to worship in a charismatic manner to insist you and the majority of your congregation reshape your worship style and needs to meet theirs."

Our conversation continued for a good bit longer. I wish I could say Dad and I reached some place of common agreement. But we didn't.

Over the weeks and months that then unfolded, the tensions only increased within the congregation. The men who headed the small handful of charismatic families continued to press me on their insistence I should resign, allowing for the calling of "a more fit, Spirit-filled pastor" to succeed me.

Then it happened. One after another, those families disappeared from our Sunday worshipping fellowship. When I inquired of them, they each informed me they had decided to attend the charismatic congregation several miles away—the same one to which my father had recommended I urge the families to move their membership.

Over the years I confess to countless times when I've revisited my backyard conversation with Dad, asking myself which of us was "right." And each time I do so, I find myself wondering if that question is answerable. I still believe deeply in God's design and desire for the unity of the entire church—and therefore of each and every congregation. But as distressing to me as my late father's simple, pastoral counsel was—to recommend to my discouraged parishioners to leave and find a new church home—it ended up being prophetic.

Regardless of whether or not Dad or I could be proven to be "right," what remains unarguable is this. The church is broken. As broken as each and every one of us is. Yet I believe without reservation—as I most assuredly believe my late father would, as well—that brokenness will be healed. The church, along with all creation, will know the restorative, unifying touch of Christ's healing grace just over the human horizon. In *that* day we will be made one.

How I yearn for that day.

22

Pillars and Salt

With quiet pomposity, Theodore chuckled over the phone, saying, "Oh, she can wait, I'm sure." Before I could respond, he added, "I'm at home in my study. You'll find me here as soon as you drive over." Click.

I had been sitting at my desk, just five minutes prior to my intended departure for a home visit with Louisa, a single mother in our congregation. On her request she and I had scheduled the informal home visit a few days earlier. I had planned my pastoral call to work around her frenetic schedule of dental appointment, housecleaning, grocery shopping, and picking up her four year old from the preschool program at a nearby church.

Just prior to grabbing my coat and heading off to see Louisa, the phone rang in my study. It was Theodore, a retired member of my congregation. "Mornin', Bob. I've got some important church business to discuss with you." He then directed—not invited—me to drive over to his home so he could "get (me) up to speed about some fiscal concerns" he had about the congregation's annual budget design.

"Thanks for the invite, Theodore," I managed to say. "But I have a home visit I'm off to momentarily."

"Who's it with?" he asked.

So unprepared for his prying question, I stupidly responded. "Well, I'm going to see Louisa Smith." As soon as I did so, I regretted it. I thought to myself, "What business is it of his to ask me? And how come I so quickly told him?" I confess to feeling both irritation and shame. Irritation I had allowed Theodore to demand information he had no right to expect. And shame I had succumbed to his presumed position of privilege to demand it of me.

Before I collected my disturbed thoughts and sorted out my distressed feelings, Theodore did his chuckling thing. He said with unapologetic certainty, "Oh, she can wait, I'm sure. I'm at home in my study. You'll find me here as soon as you drive over." And then the harshest sound of all: click.

I sat there, fuming and deflated.

But that's when memory of my conversation with Grandpa, well more than two decades earlier, began to work its way to the surface.

My late mother's beloved father was a dear soul. He had served several parishes as a highly regarded pastor, and had then retired with Grandma in the town where they had attended college—the same institution where I would do my own undergraduate studies some six decades later. During my college years, Grandpa lived just a few blocks from the campus in a one floor duplex into which he had moved after Grandma sadly had passed away. I would walk over to his small apartment almost weekly, laundry bag in tow. While the washer and dryer did their thing, he and I would chat, watch a game on TV, and simply enjoy each other's quiet company. But during my senior year his health failed precipitously, leading to his admission into a nearby nursing home. Though our visits then became less frequent, they were no less meaningful.

It was during one of the last of those chats I ever had with Grandpa that he offered to me the counsel that came to mind years later in the wake of Theodore's phone call.

Lying in his nursing home bed, Grandpa had taken my hand in his, and then said, "So, you're thinking about going into the ministry?" On his earlier inquiry I had explained I was giving serious consideration either to do doctoral work in Arabic studies or to do seminary preparation for ordained ministry. He had nodded with interest, and then announced without preamble, "Well, if you end up going into the ministry, there are two things you'll need to remember."

Not having requested any advice from him, I wasn't sure how to respond. Attempting to be gracious, I asked, "What two things do you have in mind, Grandpa?"

Still holding my hand in his, he glanced up at the ceiling for a quiet moment, and then looked straight into my eyes. With determination he said, "Never let the pillars get in the way. And never stop calling."

I confess I had no idea what he meant. None whatsoever. "Never let the pillars get in the way? And never stop calling?" I asked.

"That's right," he responded.

I waited for clarification. When none was immediately forthcoming, I inquired as gently as possible, "What do you mean, Grandpa?"

He smiled, somewhat ruefully. "Well, Bob, you'll find in every parish where you might end up being the pastor, that there are folks who think of themselves as the pillars of the church." I nodded, not sure if I was following his imagery. "Those folks are the ones who think they hold up the church. They're the so-called pillars who presume it's they, and their money and prestige, that keep the church from collapsing. They think everyone else needs them, period." I nodded again, now beginning to track his metaphor a bit better. He continued. "But those folks who think of themselves as the pillars? They're not the ones who'll need you the most. In fact, the ones who'll need you as their pastor are the ones in the corners of the church, so to speak. You'll need to pay attention to them, since most of the so-called pillars don't." Then he smiled, but said with undiluted intensity, "You'll need to walk around those pillars to be sure to get to the ones who really need you." Quietly he added, "Those in the corner? They're the salt of the earth (see Matthew 5:13). They're the ones from whom the church draws its most strength." He teared up, saying, "It's the salt of the earth who will need you the most. And just as importantly, you'll discover you need them the most, as well."

I nodded, trying valiantly to follow all he was saying.

"So, never let the pillars get in my way, Grandpa? Instead, remember the salt of the earth?"

"Exactly," Grandpa responded. He lay still, looking at the ceiling pensively.

"And then you said to never stop calling?"

"That's right."

"What do you mean, Grandpa?" I once again queried.

"Well, Bob, a pastor's job—no, a pastor's privilege—is to call on parishioners. To visit each and every one." Beginning to understand what he was saying, I nodded. He continued. "It's a pastor's job to do that every day, all year long." I nodded again. "It's a pastor's job to do that from beginning to end." He paused, and then said, "Never stop calling. Especially on the salt of the earth—the ones the pillars think they're so much better than. The salt of the earth deserve your attention, maybe more than those crazy old pillars."

Grandpa stopped talking. I sensed it was time simply to let his words, his images, and his wisdom make their home in my heart. Which is what I did.

Now, more than twenty years later, Grandpa's wise pastoral counsel came vividly into focus. I realized he had been warning me about moments when the Theodores of my pastoral story would jauntily insist on my time, even—maybe especially—if that meant the Louisas of that same story would have to wait in line. Theodore the Pillar had made it clear Louisa the Salt would understand the ecclesiastical order of things. The pillar in the center presumptively expected his pastor to ignore the salt in the corner. Grandpa was being proven right.

I sat at my desk for a few minutes, then looked up at the wall on the far side of my study. There hung three photos from eons ago, and yet alive for this very moment: pictures of my father, as well as of each of my grandfathers, all three esteemed pastors. But it was my maternal grandfather who in this instance most knowingly looked me in the eye and provided me with renewed pastoral perspective and determination.

I then picked up the phone, dialed Theodore, and informed him I would come by in due course. But Louisa and I needed to visit—right now. He harrumphed a bit over the line, somewhat irked and definitely confused. I opted in that moment not to engage in discussion over the phone about pillars and salt; that time might come soon enough. But in this moment I simply said, "It's time for me to call on Louisa."

Thank you, Grandpa.

23

Decisions, Decisions

I WAS STANDING IN front of the mirror, buttoning up my preaching robe. It was time for me to head from my study up the stairs and into the sanctuary. The organist was in place, awaiting my arrival in order to begin the worship hour with her prelude. Then the unexpected occurred.

There was a knock on my study door. It wasn't a light tap, but a sharp rap that suggested urgency. I stepped from the mirror to the door, opened it, and saw a member of the congregation standing there. "Hi, Lorraine," I said.

She nodded and said, "Good morning, Pastor Bob. I just wanted to let you know what I think you need to do."

Clueless as to what she had in mind, I asked, "How do you mean, Lorraine?" I then made an obvious glance at the clock on the wall, feeling no small measure of time constraint, given the worship hour's imminent arrival.

"Well, I've been thinking a lot, and I decided to tell you that you should just go ahead and make the decision." I blinked dumbly, shaking my head in confusion. "You know, Pastor Bob. The decision about the Sunday school curriculum for this coming fall." Her expression was one of unfiltered conviction. It was as though her look was conveying to me, "Come on. You know what I'm talking about."

I did, but I didn't.

For several months our congregation's Christian education committee had been engaged in a prolonged process of discernment. They were attempting to finalize a recommendation to the congregation's governing board what the coming fall's Sunday school curriculum should be. Prior to finalizing that recommendation, the committee had thought it best to schedule opportunities for congregational input, especially from parents of Sunday school children and from likely Sunday school teachers and volunteers. On three separate occasions that input had been received as part of lengthy open meetings, during which a host of suggestions were shared and discussed. The upshot was a surprisingly complex set of issues that had made the decision-making process somewhat more challenging than anticipated. Overall, the dialogues had been constructive, albeit still unfinished.

Lorraine, a mother of three children in the Sunday school, had shared in the various conversations about the preferred curriculum. Her contributions had been insightful and helpful. Now here she stood in my study doorway, essentially blocking my path up to the sanctuary for worship.

"Uh, Lorraine, I'm actually not sure what you're talking about. What do you mean that I should go ahead and make the decision?" I glanced again at the clock.

"Well, Pastor Bob, you're the priest. It's your call. You should make the decision, since you've heard from all of us. It's your decision to make, and it's time you make it and let everyone know."

"I'm the priest?" I thought to myself. *Oh.*

That's when it began to make some sense to me.

Lorraine had married a member of the congregation I was serving—a Reformed church. But she had done so as a daughter of the Roman Catholic church, having been raised in an ecclesiastical setting defined by the prominent role of the priest. The contrast in responsibilities and decision-making privileges could not be greater between the Reformed and Roman Catholic churches. In the Reformed church, most decisions—such as what Sunday school curriculum to use—lie in the collective hands of the elected elders and deacons from the congregation. Not so in the Roman Catholic church. Rather, in the latter it is essentially the priest—and solely the priest—who makes the call about virtually all matters. Lorraine had been raised in a church context defined by the role of the priest, who oftentimes far more efficiently made decisions that otherwise would take much longer if left in the hands of groups of church members.

Now a part of a Reformed church, Lorraine remembered all too well how much more efficiently decisions had been made in her church of origin. She rightly recognized that when the decisions had been made by the priest, the congregation had accepted them and moved on, more often than not with a spirit of acceptance. Now, however, she had come face to face with the oddity—not to mention the seeming inefficiency—of a slower, somewhat democratic decision-making institution. And she was understandably wearying of it.

For good reason she had knocked on my door and declared what to her was not only the self-evident, but also the more efficient. "You're the priest. It's your call. You should make the decision, since you've heard from all of us. It's your decision to make, and it's time you make it and let everyone know."

I smiled as soon as I thought silently to myself, "I'm the priest?" I sincerely hope the smile was both warm and respectful. "Lorraine, please understand. I'm the pastor. But I'm not a priest. I don't make decisions the way a priest in the Catholic church is expected to." She stared at me, looking a bit befuddled. I said, "In our congregation it's not up to the pastor. It's up to the elected elders and deacons, together, to decide."

To which she responded with a shake of the head, "That doesn't make sense. This process we're going through is exhausting." I nodded. "I think we'd all be better off if *you* simply decided and then announced what you've decided." Now I didn't nod. "Everybody would be fine with your decision, and we wouldn't be so tied up in knots with this process of making decisions as a group." Before I had the chance to respond, Lorraine shrugged and said, "Well, I should let you go. It's time for church." With that, she turned and headed up the stairs to the sanctuary, followed by her pastor. Not her priest.

I've recalled that fascinating exchange with Lorraine on many occasions over the years. In one sense, it helpfully revealed a perspective many of the members of the congregation I was serving may have shared with her. A sizeable number of the members, like Lorraine, had roots in the Roman Catholic church—far more, in fact, than had roots in the Reformed church. Their experience growing up in a church setting defined, therefore, by a priest's leadership was one that could not—nor should not—be ignored. On any number of occasions it became clear that those raised in the Roman Catholic church seemed inclined to await my thoughts prior to sharing their own. Not so with those raised in various Protestant churches, including the Reformed church. On more than one occasion, after that brief exchange with Lorraine, I found myself quicker to spot the various instances where members approached deliberative meetings with very contrasting perspectives on the decision-making process. Being aware of those instances became an essential factor in my trying patiently to provide those groups of church members with the support required for the hard work of debate and decision.

A final word. Over the years I confess to many a moment when I've had to look in the mirror, not to button my preaching robe but to acknowledge the peculiar dynamics of serving as a pastor, not as a priest. On countless occasions I have looked myself in the eye and had to ask, "Am I remaining true to the role of pastor, or have I allowed the congregation quietly to nudge me in the direction of priestly authority?" While affirming the office of pastor—minister of Word and Sacrament—as one understood to incorporate the roles of prophet and priest, have I given subtle permission to the members of the congregation to echo dear Lorraine's Roman Catholic voice? Have I allowed them, on convenient occasion, to allow me to assume a position of authority I claim not to have, but which when used in subtle manner may absolve the congregation of its rightful—and yes, demanding—decision-making responsibility?

Even well into my years of retirement, I remain unsure how to answer the questions above. It may be my uncertainty is rooted in the mystery of the church itself, or at least in the vagaries of the church's institutional ways. Maybe I'm unsure how to answer the questions above because the institutional church is a muddled body, with no one model of pastoral leadership and congregational decision-making ultimately superior to any other.

Until any clarity about my befuddlement may surface, I remain grateful for—and humbled to walk alongside of—Lorraine and every one of her sisters and brothers who comprise the church, both locally and eternally.

24

Issues

It's an expression—sometimes an accusation—that's been around for longer than I can remember: "You've got issues." And as most of us can well attest, variations on that expression are innumerable. "She's got issues." "He's got issues." "They've got issues." "We all have issues."

But the variation that's undeniable for me? "*I've* got issues."

Over the years I've had the opportunity to acknowledge—yes, to confess—I have countless issues that have impacted who I am and how I live. That truth applies, I sincerely believe, to each and every one of God's children, no matter our history, our family, our personality, our what-have-you. We each have powerful dynamics in our life story that can be, and *need* to be, recognized and addressed. Absent such recognition and address, those issues will surface again and again, catalyzing innumerable, often immobilizing results.

Such was incontestably the case for me when I stood, robed to the max, in front of my father and his bride.

The year was 1988. It was early in January, ten years and only a handful of days since my mother's having succumbed to cancer in 1977. During the first several years following Mom's passing at the age of fifty-six, my older siblings and I had begun to drop barely disguised hints to Dad that he was still a relatively young widower. Why not allow himself to date, with the possibility God might introduce him to someone with whom he could spend together what would hopefully be a significant number of years? Dad, bless his gracious heart, expressed his appreciation for our urgings, but seemed utterly to ignore our counsel.

However, in due course Connie entered his life. The widow of a pastor, she began to date our father, himself a pastor. After some time, they became engaged. My siblings and I were happy for him, and looked forward to celebrating the next phase of his life with Connie.

Somewhat to my surprise, Dad and Connie asked me to officiate at their wedding service. Though by then in my pastoral career I had officiated at dozens of weddings, this one, for self-evident reasons, felt different. But I accepted their invitation, honored to have been asked.

As the wedding day approached, I prepared myself for the unique privilege of standing before Dad and Connie, guiding them through the liturgy, culminating in their exchange of wedding vows. The evening before the service, they and I, along with the wedding party and family members, walked through the liturgy. Ironing out all the details as best we could, we then headed off to the rehearsal dinner, all smiles. That included me.

The wedding day arrived. Once I ensured all were in place, both in the pews and in the gathering space outside of the sanctuary, I signaled to the organist to begin the prelude. As that piece drew to a conclusion, I led Dad and my brother, Dad's best man, to the head of the center aisle. On cue, the processional music then began. Connie's bridal attendant led the way, followed by Connie on her own son's arm. All rose as the two of them walked towards the front. Smiles abounded. All seemed in order. A decade and two weeks since Dad had lost Mom, there Dad stood, prepared to commit his love and faithfulness to Connie. Timed beautifully with the organist, Connie and her son arrived up front, just a foot or two in front of Dad. And of me.

The music ended. I invited the congregation to be seated. I looked down at my liturgy book, ensuring I was prepared to read clearly and steadily. But then, just before I intoned "Dearly beloved, we are gathered together," it happened. I looked over the top edge of my book, and I happened to spot the shoes on Connie's feet. At which point I found myself thinking, with no small measure of intensity, "*Mom's* supposed to be in those shoes!" I said nothing aloud. But in that silence, my thoughts broiled: "*Mom* should be standing there!"

Thankfully, my good and understanding Lord deadened my lips for an instant. Even had I wanted to blurt out loud the insanity I was thinking in that moment, God ensured I did no such disruptive thing. Within two or three seconds—which felt like two or three hours, to be honest—I managed to say, "Dearly beloved, we are gathered together . . ." And while doing so, my heart and my head conferred. Their mutual diagnosis? "It's your issue, Bob. Not Dad's. Not Connie's. Not even Mom's. It's *your* issue." And with that, my heart and head agreed to address this issue at a later date, far, far away from there and then.

It was my issue, no one else's. It just so happened that it took standing there at the head of the aisle, readied to guide Dad and Connie through their marital promises, that I was forced, thank God, to acknowledge it as such.

Later that evening, after returning to the hotel room, I shared the above with my ever patient and always insightful wife. With her gentle assurance, I took solace in that I had not betrayed what my explosive thoughts had entailed earlier that day. But on my wife's equally gentle encouragement, I made a resolution. Sometime in the immediate future, I realized I needed to find a place and time to examine that part of me that had clearly not done an honest inquiry into my dear mother's passing a full decade earlier. I realized I needed to name my issues, and to give appropriate consideration to how those issues remained, albeit suppressed and unacknowledged all these years later.

I had issues. And I've still got them, as do we all.

In the several decades since that moment staring in shock at Connie's shoes, I confess I've found myself increasingly aware of issues I've thought I'd well addressed, but haven't in any meaningful way. My issues run the gamut, as I suspect is the case for, oh, everyone. Like me, yours may have to do with parent/child relations, or maybe with spousal tensions or co-worker conflicts. They may have to do with experiences of pain or loss in a church, in a school, or in a community. They may have to do with injurious traumas as a child, as an adolescent, or as an adult. Whatever those issues may be, they remain silently in place and in play until and unless they are named and examined.

As a pastor, I can attest to countless instances over the years when one or another individual has said in my presence, "Oh my word, I thought I'd dealt with that years ago! But here it is!" Then, "Pastor Bob, I've got issues!"

To which, in one pastoral way or another, I've oftentimes responded, "You, too?" And then, "Jack/Jill, we all have issues. And though we may be aware of some of them, it's almost guaranteed, in my estimation, we each have issues we're not at all aware of until they make themselves evident in the most unexpected ways." Such as at weddings, I'm often tempted to add.

Though it still causes me a bit of a gulp, if not a missed heartbeat, to remember so vividly what it was like to look at Mom's—oops, Connie's—shoes, it remains essential for me to remember. It remains crucial I allow those surprising moments to be the gifts they are: opportunities to spot my issues and commit to examine them. For issues that go unspotted and unexamined remain. They disrupt and immobilize. But issues dealt with in honesty and vulnerability become opportunities for healing. For hope. Even for life.

25

Whisper

OVER THE YEARS I've come to realize Ray Kinsella and I are spiritual kin. I suspect I'm not alone in that regard. I think it likely many of us—maybe even you—would recognize ourselves in that fictional corn farmer whose life had a moment when he heard a whisper he was unable to ignore.

Ray Kinsella, in case you're unfamiliar with him, is the central character in the 1989 fantasy drama film entitled "Field of Dreams" (itself based on W.P. Kinsella's 1982 novel *Shoeless Joe*). I'll not attempt to retell the movie's full and complex plot, but for my purposes here I'll share the following, which ultimately led to my feeling unanticipated kinship with Ray.

The Kinsella family of Ray and Annie, as well as their young daughter Karin, live on a farm in Dyersville, Iowa. One day, while walking through some of the tall rows of maturing corn, Ray hears a whisper, promising him, "If you build it, he will come." Understandably, Ray is dumbfounded. He has no idea who's communicating with him, nor what on earth the whispered declaration signifies. The balance of the film's unfolding story line leads him to do what strikes many others, apart from his ever-patient wife, as sheer insanity. He uproots several acres of precious cropland, corn and all, and builds a full-size baseball field. By the film's conclusion, the whispered promise comes true, absolutely unforeseen by Ray. His late father, with whom he had had a rocky relationship in his youth, comes forth. Along with countless other ball players from decades earlier, Ray's father walks quietly out of the rows of corn—and out of the past. Ray and his father end up meeting, talking, playing catch, and beginning to experience the blessing of long overdue restoration and affection. In the end, because Ray has heard the whispered instruction to build the field of his dreams, he and his father are made whole.

If you've not seen the film, I heartily recommend it. Appearances to the contrary, it's clearly less a film about sports, and more one about the blessing of healed relationships. And as an aside, I wager most of the film's viewers find the theme music profoundly soul-stirring. I certainly do.

Well, what of that spiritual kinship to which I alluded above? It's that sense of being brothers with Ray Kinsella I've found to be deeply resonant over the past three decades. You see, like Ray I heard a whisper one day. And that whisper led me, too, to my father.

It was the summer of 1989. Dad had passed away that spring, having battled cancer for several years. Mom, too, had succumbed to cancer a dozen years prior to Dad. In May I had shared in the process of coordinating Dad's memorial service in California and subsequent service and burial in New Jersey. I had then returned to my own ministry in upstate New York.

Then that summer I heard the whisper.

It was a late, midweek afternoon. I was driving the sixteen miles home from a hospital visit in Albany. As was my wont, I was listening to the upstate New York radio station that plays classical music. Some ten minutes before driving into our home village, it happened. A piano and orchestra piece played out—one I had no memory of ever hearing before that day. It's not overstatement to say that piece grabbed my heart. I found myself inexplicably tearing up, both in sorrow and in joy. When the piece concluded, the radio host said in his typically monotonic manner, "That was Rachmaninoff's 'Rhapsody on a Theme of Paganini,' Opus 43." As soon as he noted that in his understated way, I found myself hitting the car brakes and pulling to the side of the country road on which I was driving. Once the car was still, I grabbed my pen and found a clean, unused napkin from an earlier McDonald's order. I rapidly jotted down the music's title. But as I was doing so, the radio host continued, now with an atypical tone of almost playful delight. "For those of you who are movie buffs, you'll recognize this Rachmaninoff piece as central to the 1980 film 'Somewhere in Time.'" That was it. He said nothing more. In fact, as so often is the case with public radio classical music hosts, he then remained silent for maybe five or ten seconds, prior to introducing the next piece to be played. During that silence I found myself writing "Somewhere in Time" on that same napkin.

That was the whisper moment.

I sat in the car, alone on that quiet road, and realized I needed to follow up on what I had just heard and learned. I needed to listen again to Rachmaninoff's gorgeous composition. But additionally, I somehow knew

I needed to watch that nearly decade old movie. A movie I had never heard of before.

After wiping tears from my cheeks, I put the car back in gear and drove on home. I recall sitting that evening at the kitchen table with my wife, describing my afternoon experience. At the conclusion I said, "I have to rent that movie." Mary smiled gently and nodded, though likely somewhat unsure what indeed had happened to her husband back on that roadside.

Saturday night arrived. With our young daughters soundly in bed upstairs, Mary and I planted ourselves on the living room couch. With a peculiar eagerness, as well as an uncertainty about what lay in store, I put the clunky tape of "Somewhere in Time" into our well-used VHS player, turned on the TV, and hit "Play." For the next hour and a half we watched the story unfold on screen. In all truthfulness, the quality of the movie was less than stellar.

Still, Mary and I watched, enjoying the Rachmaninoff piece's melodic background. The story line unfolded. For those who have never seen the film, the plot is as fantasy-based as that of "Field of Dreams." In brief, the main character, Richard, happens upon a painting of Elise, an actress who lived (and died) decades before Richard. Richard is enamored of Elise, becoming obsessed with being able to meet her. With the aid of a friend who coaches him on the capacity for self-hypnosis to help one travel back in time, Richard astonishingly goes back to Elise's era, meets her, and the two fall in love. But in due course, Richard's hypnotic travels are upended, he returns to the present day, and finds that Elise is absent, having passed away years ago. As the movie heads to its conclusion, Richard's aching heart takes center stage. The viewer—including me, as I sat on the couch with Mary—yearns for Richard and Elise to be reunited.

It was then, while watching the final few minutes of this at times ponderously slow-moving story, it happened. In the final scene of the film, Richard does the unexpected. Lying down, he wills himself to travel. Not back in time, but forward. From this life to the next. He chooses, in a mysterious way, to end his lonely life here, in order to be reunited with Elise in paradise. Sure enough, as Rachmaninoff's piece explodes in unmitigated splendor on the sound track, Richard and Elise are once again together. Not just for a brief day or two, but for eternity.

Sitting on the couch, I confess to that point in time beginning to wonder why I had been so drawn to watch this mid-quality, fantasy romance. It then hit me. As my wonderful wife can still attest, the tears erupted. "*Dad and Mom* are together again," I remember sobbing aloud. "They're *together*!"

I was overwhelmed. With joy, peace, wonder.

That's when I realized it. Just days earlier I had heard a whisper on that road coming home from the hospital, when out of the blue the "Rhapsody on a Theme of Paganini" had grabbed my soul and led me ultimately to that cinematic moment on the couch. Had led me to that moment of my gracious God assuring me, "Your parents are together, Bob. Again, and forever."

As Mary is my witness, after the movie's credits ended, I sat on the couch and wept for half an hour. And my heart began to heal.

Some years later, while watching "Field of Dreams" for the first time, I realized Ray Kinsella and I are spiritual kin. We are brothers, each having been given the unsolicited gift of a divine whisper. That whisper, though breathlessly silent to others, enabled each of us to meet our father (see 1 Kings 19:11–12).

Can I explain any of the above in unarguable, scientific terms? Of course not. If you find yourself unconvinced, bemused, or even concerned for my cognitive well-being, that's fine. I'll allow you whatever uncertainties you may have about me. But please know for me the whisper was undeniable. Impossible to ignore. And I, like Ray, have been the better for hearing it and going where it led me. To my father. And to my mother.

I invite you to listen to your whisper, whenever and wherever it may find you, as well.

26

Counterintuitive

ENSURING I WASN'T MISREADING his counsel, I said, "You're not joking, I gather."

"No, not at all," responded Geoffrey. "I'm very serious."

I nodded, albeit mutely, trying to process what he had just shared with me.

I was sitting in the study of my dear friend and peer in pastoral ministry. Geoffrey was about eight years my elder, currently serving as a senior staff person in one of my denomination's regional synod offices. When I had called him a day earlier, he did as I guessed—and hoped—he would do. He invited me to make the forty minute drive to see him in person.

Our subsequent face to face conversation had been precipitated by a flurry of phone conversations that had unfolded over the previous three weeks. I had been contacted by the chair of a pastoral search committee of a fairly large and well-known congregation some two hundred miles south of the village of the wonderful congregation I had been pastoring for a decade.

During those exchanges with the search committee chair I was informed his committee was very interested in having me engage in conversation with them about the possibility of their recommending that I be called as their congregation's next senior pastor. While that information was somewhat humbling, I found myself unsettled by it. Why? Because I was not at all of a mind to be moving from one parish to another at that point in time. To the contrary, I had been deepening in my sense of call to remain the pastor where I had been for the past ten years. Though some of my peers wondered aloud with me from time to time if I might be ready to start looking for a new congregation to serve, I invariably responded with, "No. I feel this is where I'm meant to remain, at least for a few more years."

Then came the initial phone conversation with the search committee chair, followed by several more over the next couple of weeks. He was gracious but insistent, indicating the committee was feeling compelled to press me to give prayerful consideration to have a face to face visit with them.

In due course my wife and I discussed at some length what I should do. The upshot of our deliberation? I called Geoffrey, with whom for several years I had become accustomed to consult about all things ministerial. Hence his invitation to see him the following day.

Now in his study, door closed, I described the several weeks of phone calls and my uncertainty about what to do. Geoffrey then led with a quiet, "Describe for me what you're unsure about, Bob."

"Well, I'm not looking to move. I'm a decade into my ministry up here, and the idea of moving two hundred miles south, starting anew with another congregation, feels odd if not wrong." He nodded, remaining silent. "And there's no question a move now would be monumental for my family." Again he nodded. "So I'm inclined to tell the search committee chair, 'Thanks, but no thanks.'"

It was at that point I seriously expected Geoffrey would smile and intone some variation of "Well, there you go." But was that expectation ever wrong.

"Well," began Geoffrey, "it seems to me you need to drive down there and have an in-person interview with the committee."

He stopped, and I stared. "You think I should go down there? Even when I just said I'm inclined to tell them 'no thanks'?" My voice had risen a full octave, betraying my surprise.

"Yes," he responded. "No question about it."

Ensuring I wasn't misreading his counsel, I said, "You're not joking, I gather."

"No, not at all," responded Geoffrey. "I'm very serious."

I nodded, albeit mutely, trying to process what he had just shared with me. Acknowledging my befuddlement, he continued. "Over the years, Bob, I've discovered something that feels counterintuitive, but is true nonetheless. When it comes to the hard-to-define process of discerning a call from God, it's become increasingly clear to me that process requires testing instances when I may not yet be aware of a call." He stopped, noting my look of curiosity, if not confusion. "In your instance, for example, you've not been sensing any call to move from your current parish to another. And that's fine. In fact, that's encouraging, because it suggests your pastoral relationship with your parish remains positive and nourishing. But that doesn't mean God doesn't have other work to which you are possibly meant to move in the near future." I continued to look him in the eye. "It's possible—not definite, but possible—you're meant to be moving soon, even if you're not currently feeling such a call. It's possible God is letting you know through the search committee two hundred miles south of here."

"So in order to test the waters, you're saying I should seriously consider driving down there for an interview?"

"That's right. That experience will hopefully serve both you and the search committee well. There may be warm attraction, which in turn may suggest God is calling you to move. Or there may not be, in which case the interview becomes a means of reaffirming your sense of call to remain where you are."

"Huh," I said quietly. "So it might help me to know I'm supposed to stay, by going for an interview about possibly moving?" He smiled. I don't recall mirroring his smile. To the contrary I found myself swimming in uncharted territory, realizing his advice was touching on the unarguable mystery that encompasses the human process of making a decision. On the indescribable enigma that defines the pastoral venture of discerning a call.

That evening, after quiet conversation with my wife, I called the search committee chair. Plans came together for an overnight visit within the next weeks.

On arrival in the town two hundred miles south, we toured about. I then met with the committee, while my wife and our three children occupied themselves elsewhere. The interview was stimulating and illuminating. Questions were posed, answers given. On the surface there was much about the congregation's vision for ministry that resonated with my own such vision. Appearances would suggest my serving as their next pastor was a fitting match, beneficial to both parties.

After parting ways with the committee members, I joined my family in the minivan and we headed off to a nearby motel for sleep prior to our drive homeward the next morning.

Sleep came only fitfully for me. After breakfast, we piled into the minivan and headed north. The kids played quietly in the back. As the miles unfolded, my wife and I began to process all the previous twenty-four hours had brought to light. I spelled out in significant detail the host of items on the check-off list of "positives" were I to accept a call. I also noted a much shorter list of "negatives." The contrast between the two lists seemed to cry out, "It's time to move, Bob! Can't pass up this opportunity!"

But the further away from the southern parish we drove, and the closer we drew to our home up north, the more I sensed it. The more I knew it.

I was called to stay, not move.

Geoffrey's counsel proved spot-on. Whereas the visit with the search committee seemed on the surface to be proof positive I was called to move south, that same visit in fact confirmed I was meant to stay.

Which is what our family did. For two more decades of soul-nourishing life with our beloved friends in Christ.

On countless occasions over the years I've pondered Geoffrey's unanticipated advice. In any number of situations when confronted with uncertainty about a choice to be made—whatever I might be yearning to discover God's will to be—I've taken Geoffrey's counsel. I've allowed myself to investigate that which I've presumed isn't God's design for me. And time and again it's only been when I've given serious consideration to that which I've presumed *isn't* God's will for me, I've come away with clarity about what *is*.

27

Let the Children

THEY MAY HAVE BEEN only thirteen and ten, but their words—and their tears—betrayed a profundity of love from which every adult could well learn. What came to mind? Echoes of Jesus saying to his followers, "Let the children come to me, . . . for the kingdom of God belongs to such as these." (Mark 10:16)

It was the evening of one of the last days of December 1997. Three days earlier my wife and I had driven to the hospital with our son, just celebrating his seventh birthday. The trip to the medical center was precipitated by several weeks of David's radically increased intake of fluids, as well as jarring weight loss. During that daylong visit to the pediatric wing, he underwent testing that confirmed a diagnosis of Type 1 diabetes. From that day forward, for the rest of his life, he would require constant attention to his blood sugar levels and the consequent need for insulin injections.

A quarter of a century later I still recall my shock, as well as my deep distress for David. What parent would not respond in kind? Gratefully, David's new Pediatric Endocrinologist gave me and my wife Mary—coincidentally and providentially also an Endocrinologist—calming counsel and direction that caregivers of any and all young children require in order to help their children adapt to the enormously disruptive self-care that Type 1 diabetes demands. While David met in a separate room with a wonderful pediatric nurse who introduced him to finger sticks and insulin injections, Mary and I were coached in the basics of compassionate but uncompromising parenting David would need from us from that very day forward.

By late afternoon the three of us drove back home, now in possession of significant numbers of syringes and finger sticks, blood sugar monitoring equipment, and several vials of insulin. But in addition to the necessary medical supplies, we had been given significant direction about the imperative that David was henceforth required to prick his finger before every meal and bedtime in order to measure his blood sugar level, all so that he could then receive another injection of insulin into his skinny upper thigh. By that first evening of his having been diagnosed with Type 1 diabetes, I found myself numb in disbelief, calculating the staggering number of pricks and needle sticks this slim little seven year old would henceforth have to endure. I could barely contain my distress for our son, all while trying to honor his new doctor's wise insistence Mary and I approach David's care with quiet assurance and steadying encouragement.

That first evening, on the direction of his doctor, Mary and I sat with David on the living room couch. Supper awaited in the kitchen. At the kitchen table sat his amazing older sisters, Emily and Karie, patient and quiet. After the uncomfortable finger prick that enabled David, Mary, and me to assess how much insulin he would need prior to digging into his nightly plateful of mac and cheese, we filled the syringe with the requisite amount of insulin. Again on his doctor's insistence, we let David decide when to allow us to inject the insulin. Only when he said, "Okay, *now*," did we then give him his shot. As we learned over the next several days, that wait would sometimes take five, ten, even fifteen minutes. We assured him we wouldn't give it to him until he said he was ready. That assurance, however, was paired with the understanding that he, along with his sisters and parents, would not eat until he had received his insulin injection.

From that first evening on, Emily and Karie demonstrated a remarkable capacity as older siblings to wait patiently for their own meals. Not once did they complain about having to sit quietly in the kitchen until David's injection signaled it was then suppertime. Clearly they could hear all that was unfolding on the couch out in the living room. They knew in full what their beloved brother was enduring.

Which is what led to that moment that both broke—and healed—my heart. On the third night following David's diagnosis, bedtime arrived. Baths had been taken, hugs had been given, and Mary had taken David into his bedroom, where the day's final finger prick and insulin injection were now to be administered. Meanwhile, I wandered into the girls' bedroom, where they were readying for bed, as well. I sat with them for a spell, chatting quietly about their busy days. But in the background all three of us could hear the intense conversation between their brother and mother. Though the three of us could not make out the exact words being spoken in that bedroom around the corner, it was clear tears were being shed and reassuring words given in response. For a minute or two, Emily and Karie said nothing, listening in silence, but then tearing up. Which is when Emily spoke, with Karie looking on and nodding in full agreement with her older sister. "Why does David have to be going through this, Dad?" And then: "I wish it was me, instead of David."

That was it. But that was all.

I reached out to both of our daughters, embracing them with as tight a hug as I've ever given anyone. I couldn't let go. And bless their hearts, they let me hug them without a bit of resistance, somehow knowing I needed the hug as much as they.

Just thirteen and ten. That's how old they were, at least in human years. But in that moment they perfectly embodied what love is all about. It is about a willingness—even a yearning—to walk alongside those who are suffering. Or more to the point, it's about a preparedness to take the place of—and even the pain of—those who are hurting.

In that moment it was, I confess, children who revealed to me in unarguable measure what love is truly all about.

28

Blackout

THE TRUTH OF THE matter is this. *Most* of the time I haven't minded being fairly tall. And being, well, absurdly skinny. Said physical attributes allow me to help much shorter shoppers reach the top shelves when wanting the largest box of Cheerios. They enable me annually to put the star on the Christmas tree without calamitous risk of tipping all the greenery on its side. And half a century ago they meant I could lead my church's high school youth group basketball team in both blocked shots and rebounds, even though I had only limited ability to jump more than two or three inches skyward. And that's been my script ever since those adolescent years.

Of course, in addition to there being upsides to my height, there have also been challenges deriving from that same, odd physique. To wit: my poor mother, bless her soul, had to figure out where on earth she could find clothes that fit—truly fit—a five foot eleven inch frame that carried a grand total of ninety-nine pounds. That's right. Ninety-nine. Anyone want to question my mother's sainthood, given her efforts to locate a suit her sixteen-year-old son could wear to my brother's wedding that spring?

But I digress.

Most of the time I haven't minded being fairly tall and skinny. Yet there have been any number of instances where those traits have proved to be, shall we say, embarrassing at best, and compromising at worst. More often than not, they've had to do with syncope.

Syncope is the word Dr. Feldman, my pediatrician in New Jersey, insisted on using when discussing my vulnerabilities with Mom and me during my annual physical as a seventeen-year-old. "Mrs. Luidens, Robert here, being exceptionally tall and slender, is going to be vulnerable to syncope in any number of circumstances."

I remember my mother nodding in agreement. I also remember her noticing my blank expression of incomprehension, and then explaining to me, "Dr. Feldman means you may find yourself fainting on occasion." Still the blank expression. "You may find that you'll faint sometimes if the blood doesn't reach your head as quickly as it should."

"Because you're so tall," repeated Dr. Feldman, brilliant diagnostician that he was. When I nodded dumbly at both of them, he continued. "You see, Robert, you're so long, top to bottom, that the heart may have a little trouble pumping enough oxygenated blood to your brain, say when you bend over and then stand back upright too quickly. Your brain may not then get enough blood, in which case you'll possibly faint." More dumb nodding. "In those instances, you'll end up on the floor, and may wake up not remembering how you got there."

Mom, to her credit, then said, "We'll talk this over with Dad later tonight." Dr. Feldman, relieved, left it at that. As did I.

That evening my parents did indeed talk to me about syncope. About the likelihood that, unless I stood up slowly, I would faint from time to time. And not just during the next year. No, for the rest of my life.

How right they were.

Memory of two such fainting instances, in the context of my professional responsibilities as a pastor, still remain all too vivid. I confess I've tried desperately to forget both of them, but to no avail. They remain part of my long, syncopal story, shall we say.

The first unfolded on the sixth floor of a hospital in Albany. A feisty member of my parish, Leonard was a patient in room 666. (It really was 666. How could I ever forget?) He had had major knee surgery two days earlier, and was restricted to his bed, his knee held in place by a sling hanging from a rod stationed above the bed. Where normally he had a voluminous voice, he now spoke ever so softly, in no small measure due to the pain he was in—and to the meds he was on. On entering room 666, I had walked to his bedside. He noted my arrival, with furrowed brows betraying his significant discomfort. For maybe up to two minutes I stood low over his bed, face to face, but of necessity bent at my hip. After a relatively short verbal exchange, ending with a brief prayer, I stood upright. That was the last thing I remembered, until awakened by a nurse.

Per Dr. Feldman's warning, I had experienced syncope. I had fainted outright, thankfully collapsing far enough from Leonard's bed that I didn't entangle myself in the sling upholding his bandaged knee. According to the nurse now kneeling beside me at the foot of the bed, I had been out for only twenty to thirty seconds. Leonard had not only hit his "call" button to rush her into his room, he had counted out the seconds himself.

I vaguely recall asking the kind nurse hovering over me, "Where am I?"

"In the hospital," was her less than clarifying, albeit factual, response. "You fainted, probably after leaning over and talking to Leonard." When I nodded in bleary acknowledgment of her explanation, she said, "Maybe it would be best if you didn't lean over people that way in the future." More nodding in full agreement.

But did I learn from that instance? Heavens, no.

Some months later, in the dead of upstate New York winter, I went to see Ruby. A ninety-year-old widow who was beloved by one and all in our congregation, Ruby was a resident in a nearby nursing home. Essentially bedridden because of a host of incapacitating frailties, she was nonetheless an absolute delight to visit. She would regularly smile on my entry into her room. She would then point to the chair that always sat close beside her for the many of us who regularly stopped by for a chat, as much for our own nourishment as for hers.

On this particular occasion the room was exceptionally warm, the nursing staff having punched her thermostat upwards due to the frigid air seeping in through the nearby window. In a matter of minutes, I found myself beginning to sweat, in no small measure due to the thermal underwear I customarily wear in order to try valiantly not to freeze to death during the winter months. (Those with a comparable physique will likely understand . . .) For the better part of half an hour, Ruby and I enjoyed a lively conversation. Meanwhile I warmed up all the more. When finally the time came for me to do my pastorly thing, I stood up from my chair and took Ruby's proffered hand in mine. I then bent over her a bit in order to offer a prayer. Somewhere between "Dear Lord" and "Amen," I fainted. Outright, with no felt warning.

Once again Dr. Feldman's cautionary words came to bear. With inadequate blood making its way from my hard-pressed heart to my hard-boned skull, I flat out blacked out. In doing so, my head and shoulders landed squarely on Ruby's belly. Yup. Her belly.

Bless her, Ruby then gently called to me. I remember hearing, "Bob. Bob, wake up. You're lying on me."

As I came to, I recall opening my eyes and staring at the foot of her bed. Hearing her astonishingly calm voice, I blinked and slowly regained consciousness. Once I began to realize where I was, I found the side edge of the bed, pushed up, and settled back into the chair from which I had just risen less than a minute earlier.

To say I was numb with both shock and embarrassment would be humorous understatement. Once sitting back down and regaining my understanding of what had just occurred, I looked over at dear Ruby. Sheepishly, I should add. Then, in a manner that should not have surprised me in the least, Ruby said, "Well, that was quite something." Chuckling, she added, "I won't tell anyone if you won't." In response, I swore an oath to that effect, which she warmly acknowledged with a gracious, maternal pat on my hand.

Until this writing the only other soul who's ever known of my syncopal moment with Ruby has been my ever-patient wife. Who has graciously but persistently counseled me, echoing my parents, to please, *please* stand up slowly. Stand. Up. Slowly.

29

Shepherding

I WAS ONLY TEN years old. Though I thought I understood Dad's point about the challenge of being a shepherd, in retrospect I confess I had little to no clue. In fact, it took more than three decades before I began to make personal connection with my father's comments. I was making that connection because now in my forties I myself was feeling the weightiness of shepherding.

The year had been 1963. Living with my family in Beirut, Lebanon, I celebrated my tenth birthday that spring. Then during the subsequent summer months our little family took some day trips around Lebanon. One of those ventures was south from Beirut to the seaside town of Tyre, just a dozen miles north of the Lebanese border with the state of Israel. There we toured the remains of a Crusader fortress and other sites in the picturesque town.

It was on the return road trip north to Beirut that my father piqued my curiosity about shepherding. Driving along the seaside road we happened upon a large herd of sheep and goats. They were being guided across the road by a pair of shepherds, one looking to be Dad's age and the other mine. The twosome were walking with the herd, coaxing it to move steadily and safely from one side of the road to the other. The older one—likely a father—was up front, leading the way. The younger—just as likely his son—was trailing behind, chattering quietly in Arabic to the sheep and goats. Car and truck traffic had come to a full stop in both directions, allowing the herd to cross over safely. Watching this millennia old scene unfold before us, Dad then said from his seat up front, "What a job to be a shepherd, no?"

Not appreciating the implications in my father's comment, I recall saying from my back seat, "I'd love to be a shepherd! Pretty much nothing to do, and lots of time to enjoy the outdoors!"

To which Dad responded by swiveling in his seat, looking over his shoulder in my direction, and saying, "Actually, Bob, there are few jobs more demanding—and more essential—than being a shepherd." I'm sure my face registered confusion, if not disbelief. So Dad continued. "A shepherd has the responsibility of guiding to safety the whole herd, including each and every one. Though the herd tends to move about together, there are always individual sheep and goats who wander away from the rest. Each of them needs to be urged back into the safety of the whole. The shepherd has to keep an eye on those wanderers. Once a wandering member of the herd gets too far away, it's vulnerable to all kinds of problems."

I likely nodded quietly in the back seat, indicating agreement with my father's lesson about stewardly care of a herd. But it wasn't until another thirty years had passed that I finally began to appreciate Dad's wise, even biblical insight. Only then did I begin to feel the urgency, the weighty responsibility, of the shepherding vocation. And the context for making that connection? Premarital counseling, of all things.

During the mid-1970s, when my fiancée and I prepared for our impending marriage, we had engaged in brief but helpful premarital conversation with a pastor. But we each had any number of informal exchanges about marriage with other individuals, as well. They included relatives, former college roommates, co-workers, and fellow students in medical school and seminary. In each of those conversations my fiancée and I listened carefully, taking to heart the suggestions, the warnings, the advice being shared with us by those who cared deeply for us and our future marital wellbeing. We did so, in no small measure, because we understood doing so to be an expectation both of our families and of the wider culture. Were a friend or a loved one to raise a word of caution about an impending marriage, the couple were expected to listen carefully, taking that word of caution to heart and examining carefully its implications.

But something happened between the mid-1970s and the early 1990s. That cultural norm of taking seriously any and all concerns raised about an impending marriage? It slowly but unarguably eroded. In fact, it essentially evaporated. By the early 1990s, a decade into my pastoral ministry, it became unsettlingly apparent to me that young couples who were preparing to exchange marriage vows regularly and blatantly ignored input from anyone.

Every year a handful of couples approached me with the request I officiate at their upcoming wedding. I would indicate a willingness to do so, but with the proviso they meet with me for extensive premarital counseling.

That process, I explained, would include our spending up to a dozen hours in conversation in my study, during which they would describe details about their families, their plans for life together, and so forth. They would be expected to fill out extensive inventories that dealt with communication styles, decision-making approaches, vocational hopes, spiritual life interests, and the like. I explained I would tentatively commit to officiating at their wedding, but only if and when all the preparatory work was accomplished in satisfactory manner. Couples readily agreed.

It was in ensuing conversations, typically in the midst of a series of two-hour blocks, I then occasionally heard unsettling comments from a couple. One or the other might offhandedly remark that someone in their lives had raised serious concerns about the couple's relationship. "My best friend from high school thinks I'm crazy being engaged to Bruce," one of them might say, rolling her eyes. "She says he's a narcissistic nut. But what does she know, right?" Or I might hear another say, "My older brother keeps telling me Juliette lies about everything. Like he can tell? Puh-lease!" In those instances what was glaringly evident was the obliteration of the norms my fiancée and I had presumed to be honorable, and even essential, back in the 1970s. Now, just a decade and a half later, engaged couples blissfully ignored, and even callously mocked, any and all concerns intended for their consideration. And what was doubly astonishing to me, their would-be officiating pastor, was their very evident presumption I too would share their staunchly oblivious attitude about concerns others were raising regarding their impending marriage.

That's when those couples, typically to their mild shock, would discover this pastor was in fact *not* of the same mind with them. To the contrary, I refused to echo their mocking chuckles or to mimic their rolled eyes. Instead, when they would share comments describing concerns others were raising with them about their intended spouse, I would immediately say, "Please tell me more." To their surprise, I remained resolute in expecting to discuss what the high school friend or the older brother had said to the bride or groom. In a gentle yet firm tone, I would explain such caring individuals often recognized enormously important issues the engaged couple were either blind to or shrugged off as insignificant. From my vantage point as pastor, the couple's opportunity—and responsibility—was to give serious consideration *now* to such concerns that were being raised by significant compatriots in their lives. Were they not to do so at this point in time, they would be forfeiting an invaluable opportunity to prepare in mature ways for the challenges awaiting them in their impending marital union.

Was doing the above easy for the couple, much less for me? In all honesty, no. More often than not, the ensuing conversations brought to light uncomfortable issues the couple had avoided to that point in their relationship. But the unpacking of those issues in the company of a supportive pastor, well prior to the exchange of wedding vows, provided opportunity for discovery of what, in due course, would likely have surfaced. Better to bring those issues to light now, than to let them lie dormant until an inopportune moment in the early years of marriage when those same issues might ambush the couple and precipitate costly distress, if not disaster.

As the years passed, I then began to realize it. My intentional, albeit draining, routine of probing pastoral conversation with engaged couples now mirrored, in a way, my father's comments decades earlier about shepherding. On that road from Tyre northward to Beirut, when I childishly had sung the praises of a shepherd's life as being free of cares and responsibilities, Dad had quietly proposed a very different picture. Noting that shepherding is demanding and essential, he had lifted up the image of the shepherd as having the capacity—and the responsibility—to draw potentially wandering sheep and goats back into the safety of the herd. Now in my pastoral study, it was my shepherding privilege to enable couples to listen to—and not to ignore—caring, voiced concerns of others from their wider fold. Were I not to do so, those couples would all too easily allow themselves—and be allowed—to wander into hazardous places, apart from the embrace of the ones who cared deeply for them.

Now in my retirement years, I find myself increasingly grateful for the shepherding *I* have received from loved ones, parishioners, and peers in ministry. Each and all have modeled what Dad gently called me to understand while we sat in that car on the road north of Tyre, waiting for the whole herd—including every single one of its sheep and goats—to be shepherded safely across the road of life.

30

How Could I Not?

It was springtime some two decades ago, but I still remember it as vividly as if it were just last week.

I was paying a pastoral call on a young mother and her two little children. Monica and her daughters were much loved members of my parish, and were enduring unbearably trying times. Monica's beloved husband had passed away very suddenly two years earlier, leaving behind a grieving—and desperately impoverished—threesome, including two preschoolers.

As I had been doing with some regularity since her husband's tragic death, I was stopping in to see how the little family was faring. When I had called a few minutes earlier, Monica had responded in her typically warm way. "Sure. Come on by, Pastor Bob. We're not going anywhere."

On arrival, the front door was open. Looking through the screen door into the living room, I saw Monica in the middle of the floor, busy with kids around her. She waved me in. On entry, I stepped gingerly around scattered toys. Monica looked up from diapering a squirming little one, pointing her chin in the direction of the cluttered couch. "Make yourself some space and have a seat, Pastor Bob." I did so, and then took in the scene before me.

I did a head count, coming up with a number well exceeding three. In addition to Monica and her two little ones, including the squirmer now getting diapered by Mommy, I quickly noted three other preschoolers, all running about with toys in hand, raising a juvenile ruckus that would've roused the entombed Lazarus. It was a lively scene.

I quickly realized I didn't recognize the additional three kids, who each gave me passing glances before continuing with their frolicking play together. I smiled at each, and then looked back at Monica, who was now patting the back side of the newly diapered tyke as he waddled into the cacophonous fray.

Pushing herself up on her knees, and then all the way upright, Monica gestured towards the nearby dining room table at one end of the living room. We grabbed seats and took in the living room now turned into a wildly entertaining playroom, five youngsters enthralled with each other's joyous company. Understandably curious, I couldn't resist asking Monica the obvious question. "Five kids today, Monica? Wow! Who are the lucky little visitors?"

Monica looked smilingly at the rowdy fivesome rushing about the room, and said, "They're Bonnie's kids." When she could tell by the look on my face that Bonnie's name was ringing no bells, she continued. "Bonnie's a neighbor friend from around the corner. She cleans houses whenever she gets a call to do so. She got an emergency request at six this morning, so she called me and asked if I could watch her kiddos until noon." She smiled at the somewhat chaotic scene playing out in front of us, and said, "So, here they are."

That's when the surprise—no, the shock—unfolded for me.

I said with a silly look on my face, "Win-win for the two of you, I guess."

"How do you mean, Pastor Bob?" she responded, with a seriousness that made appropriate mockery of my facial expression.

"Well, she gets emergency childcare help, and you generate a little extra income for your household."

To which Monica said, with a look of mild disbelief at my foolish naiveté, "Oh, I'm not getting paid for watching her children. She has less money than I have." She paused an instant, during which time the serious nature of the moment soaked into my embarrassed soul. "No, I'm simply doing this to help her out. It's a gift," she explained.

I confess I then dimwittedly asked, "How could you do this for free, given your own financial straits, Monica?"

To which that amazing—yes, Christlike—young mother responded by saying, "How could I not?"

An hour later, back in my quiet study and beginning preparation for the forthcoming Sunday's Eastertide sermon, I found myself mulling over the jarring, yet transformative, visit I had just had with Monica. I realized she was a living reminder to me of what it means to embody the heart of Jesus. What it means to put into concrete, even counter-cultural, action the essence of our loving Lord's astonishing, self-sacrificial grace.

I closed my eyes and allowed myself to consider Monica's remarkable heart of care and compassion for her equally needy friend. As I did so, a lively picture of Jesus took shape. It was a week or two after his resurrection, just a short time prior to his forthcoming ascension. Jesus was with some of his disciples, quietly teaching them and encouraging them for what lay ahead. As he did so, I envisioned one of those still starry-eyed disciples fidgeting a bit, eager to ask his risen master a nagging question. That disciple was still in a state of astonishment, bordering on disbelief, that he was actually talking in the flesh with the same man whom he had seen some days earlier dying on a cross. When Jesus paused for a few quiet moments, the disciple finally gathered himself and spoke. "Help me to understand, Lord. You allowed yourself to be betrayed by one of us, denied by one of us, abandoned by all of us, arrested by your enemies, falsely accused by the religious leaders, unjustly tortured by the Romans, crucified between two thieves, and then buried in a cold cave." The disciple stared at Jesus, who looked back at him with startling gentleness. Then the disciple asked, "How could you do all of that? How?"

As I sat quietly at my desk, eyes closed and beginning to tear up, I could hear Jesus respond to his honestly confounded follower, "How could I not?" Then, after a moment of rich silence, he continued. "That was what my abba sent me to do. And I love you. Each and every one." And after another moment—or an eternity?—he said again, "How could I not?"

Some two millennia later, I sat in my study, listening to both Monica and Jesus. I confessed with speechless humility in that moment—as I still do—that they speak for the divine. They speak for the Spirit of God and all that the Spirit has been about since that astonishing Pentecost moment in the temple when spiritual gifts were given to the newborn community of faith who would come to be known as the body of Christ. Since that Pentecost day, the same Spirit has empowered, instructed, consoled, and inspired. That same Spirit has given to God's people what we need, sometimes—maybe always?—well before we even know we need it. Just as I did with Monica, and just as that disciple did with the risen Jesus, we may well find ourselves asking our loving God, "How could you give us such gifts? How could you see fit to give us all we need, and more?"

To which our God always, always responds by saying, "I love you. How could I not?"

31

Restored

"No, Virginia, I had no idea," I managed to say. I might have seen fit to add, "Thank you for informing me," but I confess I was so surprised—even disoriented—I was close to speechless.

Virginia and I were sitting in a corner of a funeral home's expansive worship hall. Some fifty adults were standing and chatting quietly with one another throughout the hall, out of earshot of what Virginia had just told me. All of us in that space had just shared in an hour-long memorial service on the occasion of the passing of Virginia's father-in-law, Spence. On the earlier invitation of Spence's four grown children, I had just spoken during the service about my friendship with Spence over the previous few years. Then, immediately after the host pastor had pronounced the benediction, Virginia had walked up to me near the front of the worship space and asked, "May I speak with you for a moment, Bob?" Less than two minutes later I found myself saying, or maybe just mumbling, "No, Virginia, I had no idea."

"Huh," she responded, "that's interesting."

Indeed, it was. Not just to her, but to me.

I had first met Spence about four years earlier. In his late eighties at the time, he was a resident of an assisted living facility an eight mile drive from the parish I was serving. The small room in which he lived in relative independence was adjacent to a comparable room where Zeke, an elderly member of my congregation, resided. On one occasion of my stopping in for a pastoral visit with Zeke, Zeke graciously introduced me to Spence, who invited me to stop in to visit with him, as well, whenever I would call on Zeke. I began to do so, and continued to do so even after Zeke sadly passed away.

Over the ensuing few years, on occasion I crossed paths with Spence's four offspring, who expressed delight that I was a new friend of their elderly, somewhat lonely father. Though Spence and his children, when they were growing up, were members of a congregation other than the one I was serving as pastor, that congregation's pastor, Rev. Jones, graciously welcomed my visits with Spence. "It's a win-win, Bob," noted Rev. Jones to me in one instance when we met in the hallway outside of Spence's little room. "You get to enjoy time with the old guy, and I don't have to visit him as frequently as I otherwise would."

So, for several years Spence and I came to enjoy regular chats in his quiet room. I learned of his late wife, who sadly had succumbed to heart disease at the age of eighty. He told me of his many years of work in sales, employed by a highly regarded manufacturer in the region. He proudly regaled me with vignettes about his two sons and two daughters, as well as his six grandchildren, all successes in various professions. In due course I met many members of his extended family when they would visit for holidays. His four offspring saw fit on those occasions to express kind thanks for my stopping in to see their father, allowing me in turn to let them know how much I was enjoying doing so.

Then sadly Spence's health declined precipitously. Like his late wife, his heart began to fail. He spent the last three days of his life in the ICU of a regional medical center. I went to see him a day before his passing, and visited bedside with Eric, his eldest offspring. While Spence lay in coma-like quiet, Eric saw fit to ask me if I would be willing to share a few words of eulogy at his father's likely impending funeral service. When I reminded him I was not Spence's pastor, Eric nodded in agreement, saying, "I've asked Rev. Jones if he would be okay with your speaking briefly about Dad at his funeral, and he readily agreed."

With that, I said to Eric, "Then, of course I'll do so. I'd be honored."

Spence died the next morning. Within a few hours thereafter Rev. Jones contacted me and formally invited me to share some recollections about my relatively short friendship with the elderly Spence. Four days later, I did just that. I offered to the fifty or so folks in attendance some sincere words of praise, regaling them with a few examples of the wonderful life Spence had lived as son, husband, father, and grandfather, not to mention as salesperson and friend to many. The gathered congregation listened intently, with several nods of agreement evident to me as I talked.

Then the totally unforeseen happened.

The service drew to a close. Rev. Jones offered a fitting prayer of gratitude for Spence, and closed by pronouncing the benediction. When the funeral director then hit "play" on the piped-in, recorded organ music, signaling the end of the worship hour, I stood up from my seat towards the front of the hall. My intent was to find Spence's four offspring and give them all warm hugs of consolation. But before I was able to take more than three steps in their direction, Virginia strode up to me and said, "Bob, may I speak with you for a few minutes." It was less a question than a mild demand. I nodded my willingness.

Virginia, I knew, was Eric's wife of more than forty years. Which meant, of course, she was Spence's daughter-in-law for the same span of time. She and I had visited on one or two occasions in the previous few years when I had stopped in to see Spence during one of their visits with him. She had been quiet in those instances, but nonetheless cordial in her exchanges with me. Now, in the funeral home, she directed me to two chairs in the far corner of the hall. There we took our seats, apart from the rest. Before I had even a moment to invite Virginia to begin, she asked, "Did Spence ever talk to you about raising his children?"

Entirely unsure what she may have had in mind, I responded, "Well, Virginia, he told me about all four of his children. He took great pride in their accomplishments." Then, betraying a slight degree of confusion, if not discomfort, I asked, "Why do you ask?"

Looking me straight in the eye, Virginia answered. "He probably never told you about all the ways he was verbally and emotionally abusive of Eric when Eric was growing up, did he." It wasn't a question. It was a declaration. Before I responded, Virginia continued. "You should know that my father-in-law made my husband's growing up years full of misery. Full of fear. Out of the blue, Spence would shout at his son for any little thing. For not mowing the lawn perfectly. For laughing too loudly when he was talking to his friends on the phone. For dating the wrong types of girls. Like me." On hearing those words, I found myself for a moment at a loss for any in response. "Please understand, Bob, what you shared in this past hour about Spence was fine. You knew him in the last few years of his long life. In some ways, you knew him when he had begun to look in the mirror and see himself for who he had been all those years. He came to see what a harsh, even horrible, father he had been to my husband and his siblings. And I'm grateful he had come to a better, humbler place." Then, finally beginning to tear up, she said, "But for most of his life he was a terror. To all of us—but especially to my husband. You wouldn't have known that, and that's fine. But I thought you should know now." With that, Virginia stopped, still looking me in the eye, but with tears now overflowing her own.

"No, Virginia, I had no idea," I then managed to say. I might have seen fit to add, "Thank you for informing me," but I confess I was so surprised—even disoriented—I was close to speechless.

To her inestimable credit, she reached out her hand in a manner one could rightly describe as pastoral, quite honestly. There, in the midst of her own pain, she extended her honest and compassionate self to me, who just fifteen minutes earlier had extolled for all present the seemingly unimpeachable qualities of her late father-in-law—the same one who had wounded her beloved husband for too, too many years.

For the next half hour Virginia and I talked. It was one of the most honest conversations I have ever had. It was not easy, but within it were undeniable elements of relief and healing. Virginia was extending to me the gift of unblemished honesty—the kind of honesty requisite for restoration. Did she receive any expression of grace from me during that time? I'd like to think so. But far more significantly I can attest to receiving from *her* the gift of disclosure. The necessity of revelation—including of pain that will know healing only when named rather than buried.

When we finally stood from the two chairs in our quiet confessional corner, Virginia and I gave each other a warm hug, not so much of affection as of respect. We then moved across the hall as a pair and found her beloved husband. As we approached, he looked first at me, then at his amazing wife, and then back at me. The look on his face was one of recognition. It was as though he knew instinctively what his wife had just told me. When I stood before him, he astonished me by reaching out and embracing me. I returned the hug, and we held tightly for several seconds. When we let each other go, I stood back, looked him in the eye, and said, "You have an extraordinary wife."

Looking at Virginia, and then back at me, he said, "Yes indeed." Then, revealing the depth of his perception, he said, "And Dad came to know that in the last few years." When I nodded my understanding, he added gently, "And he came to know that about me, too."

Nodding tearfully, I then shook his hand. After just a few more words, as well as another hug as a threesome, we parted ways.

Years later I continue to ponder the mysterious nature of how we humans move through this life, potential agents of both painful suffering and healing restoration. How thankful I am for each and every instance when, by God's wondrous grace, the latter wins out.

32

Service Station

I LOOKED AROUND, TAKING in the sight of that inner city food pantry. Before I realized it, the brief exchange I had had with Bert almost two decades earlier came vividly to mind.

I was now on a little tour. My guide was Clement, a member of the Roman Catholic congregation in the same village as the Reformed congregation I was serving as pastor. A week earlier Clement and I had been talking about the ministries our two village parishes helped to support, including the food pantry hosted by his Catholic parish. When I had expressed my appreciation for that modestly sized food pantry, Clement had said, "Well, Pastor Bob, if you wanna see a big time food pantry, come with me next week into downtown Albany and I'll show you firsthand."

Having accepted his invitation, I drove seven days later some twenty miles from our village into the inner city of New York's capital city. There I met Clement at the entryway to the recreation hall of a hundred and twenty-five year old, tall steepled Catholic church. For more than four decades, I quickly learned, that large congregation had hosted a daylong food pantry in their "rec hall." Every Saturday, fifty-two weeks a year, they welcomed hundreds of inner city residents to come and pick up countless bags of fresh fruits and vegetables and innumerable boxes of cereals and canned goods.

Clement and I walked into the rec hall, an oversized, aging basketball gymnasium now filled with more than a dozen long tables, all covered with grocery items. Volunteers stood behind each table, assisting those from the local neighborhood who had arrived with scores of pushcarts, backpacks, and large tote bags. Into each were being put the nourishing fare those neighbors desperately needed for their households, but were likely unable to afford in the few local stores in the inner city—or unable even to find given the dearth of anything fresh in those same stores.

Clement escorted me around the cavernous hall, introducing me to several of the volunteers, and allowing me to inhale not just the scent of the food, but the aroma of the fellowship. Many of the folks filling up their carts and bags smiled at me. Some were youngsters, clearly enthused by the prospect of chomping into a freshly harvested McIntosh apple. Others were elderly, quietly collecting the recipe items soon to be mixed into the makings of a hearty vegetable soup. The echoing conversation was rollicking, and the resulting atmosphere rejuvenating.

It was while taking in that whole scene I found myself hearkening back to my short but helpful conversation with Bert years earlier. At that moment in time my wife, our infant daughter, and I had just begun to settle into our new home, the parsonage that sat adjacent to the church building. Bert and I were chatting at the close of the church's governing board meeting he and I had just attended. Among the various topics that worked their way into our conversation was my inquiry about car maintenance. I asked Bert if he had any suggestions of good auto mechanics in the area where I could take our two cars for oil changes and such. I still recall Bert's response. "Well, Pastor Bob, I'd recommend you check out Pete Wallace's place on Main Street here in the village. That's where I take our family's vehicles." When I nodded my thanks, he smiled shyly and said, "I guess I should explain why."

"Okay, Bert," I said.

"Well, see, it's this way. There are some auto mechanic shops out there that look all spankin' clean when you walk in. But then there are others that leave a little to be desired." I nodded. "It's the ones that look a bit messy that I've come to prefer. Not the ones that are all swept up and such." At that point I'm sure my face betrayed confusion, if not disagreement. So he continued. "You see, the places that are all clean: I think sometimes they spend more time sweepin' and polishin' than they do with their heads under the hood or chassis. But that's often not the case with the shops where the floor hasn't been swept perfectly clean for more than a week, or where the shelves haven't had the oil cans put back in neat stacks that look like the pyramids in Egypt. In those kinda messier shops the mechanics, I've found, are more likely to have a keener eye when it comes to spottin' possible mechanical problems that need to be fixed."

"So you're saying I should think more seriously about car repair shops that look messier than the ones that look cleaner?" I asked, my voice betraying a modicum of disbelief.

"That's exactly what I'm sayin', Pastor Bob. That's not to say being orderly and clean is wrong. It's just to say that, in my experience, if a place looks like they haven't taken time to make everything look like your grandmother's spotless kitchen, it's probably because they know cars. And love cars. And they'll likely take real good care of yours, if you let 'em."

And guess what? My wife and I took Bert's good advice. We took our vehicles to Pete Wallace's on Main Street. Although Pete's little lobby and three stall garage always looked like they could use a good sweeping and some shelf organizing, our cars got the best care imaginable. Because Pete clearly enjoyed popping the hood, sniffing around for otherwise unseen problems before they brought unexpected calamity to our household. Under those circumstances I found myself not minding in the least wearing my old, lawn-mowing sneakers when I dropped off one of our cars.

A decade later it was my conversation with Bert that came to mind. Wandering through the old rec hall with Clement, taking in the sights and sounds of the inner city food panty, I realized I was in an ecclesiastical version of Pete Wallace's auto repair shop. The rec hall was hardly in an orderly shape. The glass in the windows was old and could well use some Windex. The paint on the walls was fading, and in places suggestive of multiple coats of various shades of grey, white, and blue. And the ceiling way above us? Even from forty feet below I could spot at least a dozen missing tiles that had evidently said to themselves, "Enough already. It's time."

But none of that, I realized, now mattered to me. Nor, I suspect, to the amazing members of the parish who made their rec hall into the life-restoring—even life-saving—food pantry for their neighbors. What mattered was their ministry, their caring, their community. Everything else—be it partly smudged windows, or multi-hued walls, or semi-compromised ceilings—evidently mattered much less.

Over the years since my conversation with Bert, and since my tour of that amazing food pantry in downtown Albany, I've wondered about the wider church. I've wondered about local parishes, be they small, medium, or large in size. I've wondered about each church being a community who typically has a building or two. I've wondered about how we within each such community tend to the care—and to the use—of our building. Do we care, sometimes, more about its appearance than its use? Do we give more attention to its cleanliness, and less to its servantly ministry to those in need?

I confess too often I've seen evidence that we the church family can be naively vulnerable to giving ourselves more to the care of our buildings than to the care of our neighbors. Would that we might take a churchly version of Bert's counsel to heart. Would that we might learn from those vibrant servants who graciously made their old church's rec hall into an urban oasis of compassion.

33

Privilege

AFTER MORE THAN TWO decades in pastoral ministry, it was a moment unlike any I had yet experienced. I handed Edward the check—the very one he had handed me a number of weeks earlier. As I did so, I explained, "The governing board expresses their thanks for your gift, but they decided it would be inappropriate to receive it, under the circumstances." The resulting expression on Edward's face was one of puzzlement. And of barely suppressed anger.

As is often the case in life, that moment arrived in the flow of a fairly long and typically complicated story.

Edward was a relatively quiet soul, in general. Retired and widowed for a good many years, he had begun to attend worship a couple of years earlier. He and I became acquainted during fairly regular pastoral visits in his home. He would describe his many adventures growing up, unabashedly outlining to me his winding pilgrimage through no small number of churches over the previous decades. In a manner suggesting I would of course appreciate it, he detailed for me his involvement in several of those congregations in surrounding communities. In each of those instances, he explained in a matter of fact manner, he had left the church when the congregation's leadership had impeded his effort to "improve their congregational life." On a few occasions I invited him to explain what he meant. "Well, you know. Things like how the organist played. Or what kind of meat cutter they used in the church kitchen. And in one of the churches, I helped them see they needed longer tables for their potlucks in the church hall." As I would listen to his anecdotal history of church shopping and hopping, I found myself beginning to wonder what element of congregational life of my own parish—and of Edward's new affiliation—he would find in need of corrective advice.

In due course I found out.

It was mid-winter. The Sunday service had ended some ten minutes earlier, and I was standing in the back of the sanctuary, greeting folks as they put on their coats and scarves and headed out the main entryway door for their drives homeward. Edward filed patiently through the line. When he finally stood before me, I extended my right arm to give him a pastoral handshake. He in turn extended his right arm towards me. But it wasn't for the purpose of shaking my hand. Instead, in his hand was a plain envelope, which he then thrust into my outstretched hand. He said, "Here." Befuddled by his action, I looked down at my hand, now holding the envelope, and read the following on it: *For new doors.* That was it.

"Good morning, Edward," I managed to say. "Thank you for this." Without much thought, I inquired, "What's this you've given me?"

Edward nodded seriously down at the envelope, and said, "Well, what it says. It's for new doors." He then pointed over my shoulder at the heavy, ten foot tall doors through which folks had traversed for well more than a century. "Those doors need to be replaced, and there's a check in there for their replacement."

Still confused, and now somewhat immobilized, I recall saying, "Oh." I then asked, "New doors?"

"Of course," he responded. "There's a bit of a draft you can feel if you put your hand up on the top left corner of the door on the right. Seems obvious that the church should get a contractor here and have him install new doors. Take out the old ones, and have him change the curved design. That's old school. The entryway needs a proper rectangular construction." He nodded down at my hand, still stuck clumsily out in front of my preaching robe, holding the envelope. "That'll be enough to cover the cost."

Before I knew what to say, Edward moved past me and out the entryway whose replacement he had just instructed me to make happen.

As fate—or providence—would have it, the wife of the chair of the congregation's building committee was the next person standing in line. She stepped forward to shake my hand, which was still holding the envelope. Pointing over her shoulder towards her husband, still in the sanctuary and conversing with several other men, she said, "Well, I wonder what Aaron will think about all of that." She smiled and frowned at the same time, patted my arm, and said, "Good luck."

Ten minutes later, noting that Aaron had left the sanctuary by a different exit door, I headed to my study to remove my robe and prepare to head home for lunch. I debated delaying the opening of Edward's envelope until Monday, but curiosity got the better of this pastoral cat. I slit open the envelope and pulled out a single sheet of paper, on which Edward had written in extensive detail the make, model, and color of doors the congregation needed to replace the existing ones. And stapled to the sheet was a handwritten check, payable to the church. For four thousand dollars.

I gasped. Then I harrumphed. Without any thought, I recall saying aloud, "Who does he think he is?"

I stared at the sheet and check, and then stuffed them back into the envelope. I headed home for Sabbath lunch and rest, choosing to leave the envelope—and my feelings—back in my study in the church.

As if that were really possible.

For the next twenty hours, try as I might, I was unable to keep from stewing about that brief exchange in the entryway to the church. I confess I was impressed by Edward's proffered generosity, but I was equally—if not more—irritated by the presumptuous implication of privilege in that moment. While a gift of four thousand dollars to a relatively small congregation was no small matter, the conditionality of said gift was unsettling at best, and angering at worst.

Come Monday morning the envelope was still sitting front and center on my desk. Uncertain what best to do with it, I decided definitively not to stick it in the church mailbox of our congregation's treasurer. Depositing it in the bank felt premature, to say the least. Instead, I called and left a voice mail message for Aaron, esteemed chair of the building committee. Within an hour he returned my call and we arranged to meet in person the following morning.

Tuesday arrived, and so did Aaron. I sat him down in my study, envelope still on my desk. I then described for him what had transpired two days earlier in the back of the sanctuary. He listened carefully. But as I detailed Edward's instructions about the necessity of replacing the church's original doors, he sat forward a bit in his chair, frowned, and said, "He thinks we need new doors?" His voice then ascended a full octave, as he added, "And he thinks he can decide for us?" When I nodded silently, Aaron sighed. "Well, let's go have a look at the doors, I guess."

The two of us headed into the sanctuary, walking from the front all the way to the back, main entryway. Aaron was quiet, evidently going through the same kind of analysis of the moment as I had two mornings earlier. For the next several minutes he examined the doors, both from the inside and the outside. We walked out to the street, and I watched as he inspected the entryway with a builder's eye. He shook his head quietly. We then headed back into the building and to my study. There, after several minutes of quiet comment, Aaron said he would bring the issue to the building committee's attention at their next meeting, already scheduled for the following week.

Two days later Edward called. "Good morning, Bob." Before I even had a moment to respond in kind, he continued. "Called a construction company yet?"

Once again caught off guard by Edward, I responded, "Well, Edward, no. I've had a brief conversation with the chair of the building committee, and he'll be bringing your offer to their regular committee meeting next week."

"Why?" interrupted Edward.

"Well, a change of this nature requires consideration, both by that committee as well as the governing board. They'll have to weigh the offer and make a decision that's appropriate for the congregation."

"No they won't," responded Edward. "I'm paying for it. The check should be more than enough to cover the cost, so there's nothing for them to discuss."

I sat in my chair, shocked. Yet not shocked.

"Actually, Edward, the decision isn't for you to make. Your gift is certainly gracious and generous. But it's ultimately up to the governing board to decide. Not you."

"What do you mean, not me?" he responded. "I'm paying for it. It's therefore up to me."

The phone conversation continued for a few more frosty minutes. I offered to continue it in person, which he reluctantly accepted. The next afternoon I sat for an hour in his home. The conversation proved of no more benefit than the previous day's phone exchange.

Over the next month, I opted to do what I rarely did. I attended two special meetings of the building committee, observing that working group's careful assessment of Edward's proposal. Uniformly the committee agreed to forward to the governing board their recommendation the existing doors not be replaced. Efficient weather stripping could and should be installed to lessen the cold air leakage. But the doors' original architectural design should be honored and retained, suggested the committee. New doors would disrupt the unique appeal of the church's original presentation.

The committee's recommendation was brought by Aaron to that month's governing board meeting. As I chaired the meeting, I was deeply moved by the thoughtfulness of all around the large table. In due course a motion was made and then carried unanimously to retain the doors as they were, along with the recommended new weather stripping. I proceeded to ask the question that hung silently but heavily in the air. "What do you, as the governing board, instruct me to do with this check for four thousand dollars?" We all sat quietly.

Then one of the deacons, who was also a member of the church's finance committee, said with quiet determination, "We should return the check to the gentleman, with thanks for his generous offer, but with clear explanation of our decision." Several folks around the table nodded quietly in agreement. "And Pastor Bob, I urge you to help Edward to understand this: donors don't make decisions for the church. It's up to the governing board to make decisions." More nods.

I could not have been more humbled—nor moved—by my sisters and brothers than I was in that quiet moment.

Two days later I again sat in Edward's living room. Per the instruction of the governing board, I handed back to Edward the check he had thrust into my hand several weeks earlier. As respectfully as possible, I explained, "The governing board expresses their thanks for your gift, but they decided it would be inappropriate to receive it, under the circumstances." His facial reaction? It was one of puzzlement—and barely suppressed anger.

I confess I hoped a reasonable conversation between the two of us would then ensue. But it didn't.

Edward reasserted his conviction that those who foot the bills should have—do have—the privilege to decide which bills to pay. No matter how much I attempted to explain the way the church's governance instructs otherwise, he dug his heels in all the more. To say we reached an ecclesiastical impasse is to indulge in comical understatement.

After the better part of two hours of intense conversation, I departed, leaving the check on the coffee table in Edward's living room.

Admittedly to my surprise, the following Sunday Edward was in attendance. This time, though, rather than sitting in his customary back pew, close to the chilly entryway, he had opted for a pew towards the front of the sanctuary. He was now planted a good distance from any cool draft finding its way through the century old doors.

Then I confess to doing that which I prided myself on refusing to do on most every other Sunday. While the offering plates were passed down the pews during the offertory anthem, I glanced in Edward's direction. I couldn't help but notice Edward passing the plate from right to left, but putting nothing therein.

34

God Rest Ye

The look on their faces was one of both confusion and relief. Dana and Connor nodded tentatively at me. I continued. "I'm serious. What you're doing on Sunday mornings is both commendable and biblical."

It was a Tuesday evening in late autumn. The three of us adults were sitting around the kitchen table, with their three children—ages four, six, and nine—playing quietly in the nearby living room. I had arrived some twenty minutes earlier, having scheduled this home visit the previous week. I had phoned their home and spoken with Dana, indicating my pastoral concern for their family's well-being. I hadn't seen any of the five of them in worship for the better part of three or four months, and expressed to her that I would enjoy a chance to catch up in person, were their busy schedule to allow for it. Dana had graciously invited me to come by at seven that next Tuesday evening, when they'd all be home.

When I arrived a few minutes past seven, Connor met me at the door of their small home. He ushered me into the living room, where I was greeted by the three kids. The two younger ones were already in their pajamas, their hair still wet from their bath time. Dana came down the stairs, having just overseen the twosome's evening wash-up routine. For a few minutes I had some back and forth chatter with all three children, hearing about school, soccer, dance, and such. When it was clear the kids wanted to be about their own games, the three of us adults retreated to the kitchen to catch up.

Once seated around the kitchen table, I invited the two parents to fill me in on how they were all faring. I indicated I had missed seeing them for some time, and was concerned that all was well with the family.

It was Connor who spoke first. "Well, Pastor Bob, we appreciate your taking the time to come by." When I nodded, he continued. "We feel kinda badly that we haven't been back to church in so long. It's not that we had any problems with Sunday School or worship, but, well, it's been really busy in our family life." He looked over at his wife.

Dana picked up where Connor left off. Referencing her own part-time work as a clerk in a local realty office, she explained, "Our jobs have gotten more and more demanding, Pastor Bob." With regard to her husband's employment in sales for a local pharmaceutical company, she said, "Connor's now been ordered to be on the road a lot more than the last few years." I looked at Connor, who continued to look at his wife. She began to tear up. "They've expanded his territory to Burlington up north, Syracuse out west, Springfield in the east, and Newburgh down south. That's a huge territory, and even if Connor's able to drive to and from one or another distribution site in one day, he's typically not home before the kids' bedtime. Sometimes he doesn't make it home until the next night." I looked over at Connor, who was now tearing up like his beloved wife.

"Wow, Connor, that sounds like a huge time demand," I said quietly. He nodded, saying nothing. Looking first at one, and then at the other, I added, "That has to be taking it out of both of you."

"You have no idea, Pastor Bob," responded Connor quietly. Sensing he had more to say, I waited. And then: "I'm around here so little from Monday through, well, Saturday, that I've been missing my family like crazy." Then looking at his wife, he added, "It's doubly hard for Dana, since she now has to do just about everything for the family, on top of her work at the agency. I used to be able to do my share of things around here, including with the kids, but that's taken a hit. In fact," he added, "this evening is the only one I'll likely be home to help put the guys to bed this week."

With that, I confess I felt a wave of embarrassment, encroaching on their limited time together as a family. "I'm sorry to take your time this evening, guys. My apologies." But before I was able to indicate my readiness to stand and make my exit, they both shook their heads as one.

"No, please don't go, Pastor Bob," said Dana. "It's really good to see you." Connor nodded in evident agreement. "We've missed everyone at the church, including you, and we're glad you haven't forgotten about us."

"You've definitely not been forgotten," I responded. Then, before I was able to say a word more, Connor looked at Dana, then at me, and spoke.

"What you should probably know, Pastor Bob, is that Dana and I decided a few months ago that Sunday mornings would be family time. Every Sunday we get up, make pancakes all together, and then play board games or read stories aloud. All five of us together in the living room." Glancing at Dana, he stopped. I waited.

Dana picked up the thread, saying, "Sunday mornings are now dear to us. Most Sunday afternoons it's off to soccer games or dance recitals, but we protect the mornings for us as a whole family." Looking down, and then back up at me, she added, "So, that's why we've not been in church on Sundays." And then, quietly, "We're sorry."

At which point I, too, teared up. I said, "No apologies are necessary. None. To the contrary, I applaud you. What the two of you—the five of you—have decided to do is commendable beyond measure."

"Are you serious?" whispered Connor. The look on both of their faces was one of both confusion and relief. Dana and Connor looked somewhat tentatively at me.

"I'm very serious. What you're doing on Sunday mornings is both commendable and biblical."

That's when I told them about a sermon I had preached ten years earlier, well before they had started to attend our congregation's Sunday morning services. I explained I had spent the better part of three months preaching a series of sermons about the Decalogue—the Ten Commandments. I noted I had read a remarkable book about those ten dictates given to the people of Israel at Mount Sinai, and what each of the ten was likely to have been understood to mean by those recently liberated slaves from Egypt well more than three millennia ago.

"The fourth commandment is about the Sabbath—what we today call Sunday. It's the commandment we typically think tells us we should go to church." Dana and Connor nodded, acknowledging that to be their understanding, as well. "Well, what I shared from the pulpit on the Sunday when we considered the fourth commandment is that that understanding misses the point. In fact, it may be wrong." The look on their faces was now one of uncertainty, if not disagreement.

I proceeded to explain the following.

"According to many Old Testament scholars, when God instructed the Israelites to 'remember the Sabbath day, to keep it holy (Exodus 20:8),' God was not commanding them to go to a gathering place in order to share in corporate worship. Rather, God was instructing them to rest. Simply to rest—with their families, at home."

While Dana and Connor listened with expressions of growing curiosity, I then described how the fourth commandment was God's gift to the previously enslaved Israelites to take at least one day each week to be together, spouses reunited and parents with children. Why? Because while in bondage, those same Israelites had been afforded no time to rest, much less be together as families. God abhorred such dehumanizing of the enslaved, now saying, "I allow—no, I insist—you spend one day each week together, not working in the field or in the market. Rest one day, at home, together as a family."

I then shared the following, with no small measure of embarrassment as a member of the clergy. "But within just one or two generations' time after the Ten Commandments had been given to the people of Israel, something grossly wrong happened. The Levites, who were the priests among the people, decided it could be to their own benefit to twist the intended meaning of the fourth commandment. Rather than simply being a gift, an instruction, for families to be reunited in rest together at home at least once each week, the priests began to teach the people something entirely different. They began to teach everyone that the fourth commandment was God's order to head, each and every one, to a high, holy place of worship. There, the priests said, men should worship with men, placing tithes into the offering plates (and conveniently into the pockets of the priests). The women, meanwhile, were segregated with each other and their children, away from husbands and fathers. The roundtrip treks to and from those high, holy places oftentimes took all day, meaning the families simply had no time to be together at home, at rest. To the contrary, they were wearied by long hikes from home to and from those high, holy places where men were separated from the rest. The end result? The intended gift of the fourth commandment was eviscerated of any blessing. In fact, the commandment was no longer a gift from God, but had been co-opted by the priestly class for their own financial and institutional benefit. And the people? Rather than be able to rest and be together as families, they were ordered to give themselves over to one more day of exhausting travel and familial separation—exactly the opposite of God's intention in the first place."

When I finished, Dana and Connor said nothing. But their faces betrayed a sense of relief, even of delight. I then said, "In my view, what the two of you have chosen to do as a family on Sunday mornings is not only wise. It's obedient. It's honoring of God's loving desire for the five of you."

"You really mean that, Pastor Bob?" Connor asked.

"Absolutely." Now both smiling and wiping some tears from my own eyes, I said, "The love the two of you are putting into action for your marriage and your children is commendable beyond measure. You are living embodiments of the fourth commandment's original intent. You are doing what God wants everyone to do: care for your marriage and your family, by resting together."

"But what about worship on Sunday mornings?" asked Dana.

"You ask a good question, Dana," I responded. "It's a question every worshiping congregation should ask together. We need to be attentive to the needs of all within the congregational family, including those such as you five who have such heavy demands on your lives the other six days of the week that you may need to consider Sunday as the day when you don't 'hike to the high, holy place,' but stay home together."

The balance of the conversation with this dear duo mirrored many such conversations I've had over the years, including several in the immediate wake of the sermon series I proffered years earlier. While I share with the wider institutional church a high value placed on regular weekly worship as a congregation, I nonetheless find myself ever in need of the corrective blessing embedded in the fourth commandment. Wherever in each congregation there may be families of any shape or size who find themselves bereft of restful time together from Monday through Saturday, it may well be the church's responsibility to permit, and even to urge, those families to "remember the Sabbath day"—to receive the God-given blessing of resting, together, as a family.

Absent the honoring of that commandment, the family of God may not only grow increasingly weary. We may grow apart, from one another and from our loving God.

35

Eulogy?

THOUGH IT WOULD HAVE been disruptive in any number of ways, I found myself in retrospect wondering whether I should still have done it. I asked myself that evening, and for several days thereafter, whether I should have gotten up in the middle of the eulogy and walked right out of the sanctuary that morning.

For several years Leonard and his wife, Libby, had been members of the congregation I served. But they had moved to a new home when offered better jobs more than an hour's drive away. They had understandably transferred their membership once they found a new congregation close to that new residence. Though they and I had kept in touch on occasion after their move, it had been several months since we had communicated with one another.

Then Leonard died in unimaginably tragic manner. While boating with Libby on a windswept lake in the Adirondack mountains, Leonard had somehow fallen overboard. Not wearing a life jacket, he reportedly flailed about for a few moments. Then, to the devastation of Libby, he slipped below the surface and drowned.

Within a day I learned of Leonard's tragic passing. I contacted Libby by phone. By that sad conversation's conclusion, she had graciously invited me to attend Leonard's funeral. On the morning of the service, a few members of my congregation drove with me to Libby's new church. On arrival, we were guided to a pew by a funeral director. We then sat through the service, just a dozen steps away from Leonard's casket, as well as from Libby and her extended family sitting in the front pew.

The service unfolded in relatively traditional manner, with quiet music and hymns, appropriate scripture readings, several prayers, and a brief word from the deceased's brother. Then the host pastor strode to the pulpit and began his eulogistic comments.

For the first several minutes the pastor spoke of the tragic loss now felt by Libby, their family, and all of us who had had the privilege of knowing Leonard. The pastor's words elicited within me a sense of profound gratitude for the time I had been able to walk alongside Leonard in our shared faith.

But then the pastor's tone changed in a palpably sobering way. "As much as we have every reason to mourn the loss of this our friend Leonard, it behooves us to address the necessary question of this moment." He stopped, looking gravely at the casket, and then at all of us in the sanctuary. "That question, I'm sure, is one Leonard would insist I ask all of us. It is this: Is Leonard now on his way to heaven, or not?"

While the pastor stopped for a dramatic moment of silence, I found myself quietly gasping. I was shocked. "'Is Leonard now on his way to heaven, or *not*?'" I echoed silently to myself.

Before I had a moment to process the essence of that jarring question, the pastor continued. "We don't know the answer, do we." It was quite evidently not a question, but a statement. "We don't know the answer because we don't know the state of his soul when he sadly fell overboard. Was he right with his God? Or not? If he was right with his God, he's heaven bound. But if he wasn't, then he's not."

The sanctuary was absolutely still, silent, as I recall it years later. Those with whom I had driven to the funeral sat beside me, equally speechless, but visibly uncomfortable. I glanced over at Libby and her loved ones in the front pew. She, along with most of the others beside her, sat forward a bit, displaying a look of confusion, if not distress.

Apparently concerned anyone might have missed the essence of what he had just said, the pastor repeated himself. "If he wasn't right with God, then he's not on his way to heaven. If his faith was not as it should be, he not only drowned. He was, and is, on his way to hell."

The congregation remained speechless, though not without some shuffling of feet and a few easily heard intakes of breath. Including from me.

Though it would have been disruptive in any number of ways, I found myself in retrospect wondering whether I should have gotten up at that point in the eulogy—eulogy?—and walked right out of the sanctuary. I confess I still don't know whether I should have done so. But I didn't. Instead, I remained in the pew, listening to the next ten or more minutes of shocking, disorienting, and yes, enraging pontificating about heaven and hell, faith and doubt, salvation and damnation. This, during a funeral for a church member whose surviving widow sat vulnerably not more than a few feet from the casket holding her late husband's body in repose.

Half an hour later, driving home with those who had kindly accompanied me, our conversation was both sad and angry. Where our earlier drive to the church had included warm recollections of Leonard and deep expressions of grief, our drive home was dominated by dismay. By a sense of offense.

Over the years since that destabilizing experience, I've frequently found myself wondering how often such a question-asking unfolds during funeral and memorial services. Though I hope I don't need to state it here, I do so nonetheless: not once during comparable funeral settings did I ever feel led—much less tempted—to pose such a question as that officiating pastor did. Not once did I ever feel it fitting to wonder aloud about the eternal condition of the deceased. And not once did it occur to me to use such a setting to instill within those in attendance comparable questions, be it about the deceased or about those mourning the loss of the deceased.

I confess—I truly believe—our gracious God yearns for us to rest in peace, not only when embalmed, but when in mourning. I believe our loving Lord desires for us to know we are in our Lord's eternal embrace—not just when living, but when dying. And when in death.

Few instances in all of scripture have captured my heart, and have framed my faith, more than that of the thief hanging beside Jesus while both were gasping for what would be some of their final earthly breaths. "Jesus," begged the crucified thief, "remember me when you come into your kingdom."

To the astonishment of that dying man, Jesus responded from the cross, "Truly I tell you, today you will be with me in paradise." (Luke 23:42-43)

While the thief had not seen fit to ask for salvation—but solely to be remembered—Jesus saw fit to assure him of the gift of eternal communion with Jesus himself.

Such is the nature of eulogy—words that are truly good. Spoken to us every day, and even—maybe especially—in the moment of our moving from this life to the next.

36

Equity

Do I know with certainty why I never heard back from them again? No. But even years later the reason seems too obvious to ignore, much less deny. It had to do with money.

I was in my late forties, one of some two dozen pastors in our regional judicatory—the conjoined collection of about twenty congregations in my denomination, all within an hour's drive of one another. For the better part of two decades I had been sharing in the oversight of those congregations. Pastors, along with elders from all of the twenty churches, were jointly tasked with ensuring healthy care was given to each and every congregation.

This work with the judicatory was above and beyond the responsibilities all of us pastors already had in serving our own individual congregations. But it was—and always has been—enormously important. Along with virtually all of my pastoral peers, I took this additional service very seriously. It included supervising seminary students from one or more of our twenty churches, assisting parishes who were searching for a new pastor, providing support to pastors who were under crushing stress, and voluntarily staffing any number of basic administrative necessities of the judicatory.

As with many other organizations—schools, service agencies, and so forth—our ecclesiastical judicatory relied upon annually elected officers to help coordinate the above efforts. During each spring meeting, nominations for a new vice president and a new president would be presented to all the pastors and elders for election to serve the following twelve months. To that end, a small nominating committee would meet ahead of time and give prayerful consideration to identifying potential nominees for those two offices.

It was that nominating committee's chairperson, Thornton, who called me mid-winter. He asked if I would be willing to meet the following week with his committee to discuss the possibility of my being nominated for election at that coming spring's meeting. Though I was not looking for one more piece to add to the list of my vocational responsibilities, I indicated to him I'd of course meet with the committee.

Six days later I drove to Thornton's church building, one of the larger facilities of the twenty or so congregations in the judicatory. I walked into the building, wound my way through a series of hallways, and ultimately into his sizeable pastoral study. The three members of the nominating committee were already sitting at a large conference table at one end of the study, and they rose to welcome me. Hands were shaken, seats were taken, and a prayer was offered by Thornton.

Little did they—or I—anticipate how the subsequent conversation would then unfold.

"Thanks for joining us, Bob," started the chairperson. When I nodded, he continued. "As you know, we're responsible for putting a slate together of two persons who will be willing to be elected as our next vice president and president. The current vice president, who normally would be elected as the next president, has indicated she won't be able to serve another year. So, we need to find two new folks to fill both of the openings this spring." I nodded again. "We'd like to nominate you to serve as president." With that, he smiled congenially. His expression betrayed a presumption such an honor would be unlikely, if not impossible, to turn down.

Sylvia, the current vice president, was a good friend and peer. During coffee a few weeks earlier she had informed me she had decided to decline transitioning from the vice presidency into the presidency in the approaching spring time. That being the case, I had driven to this meeting, anticipating the very scenario now unfolding.

"Thanks for inviting me to meet with all of you," I said to all three members of the nominating committee. "I'm humbled by your consideration of submitting my name for possible election to the presidency." All three—two men and a woman—nodded in reply. "Knowing Sylvia has decided not to be nominated to be our next president, I realized the three of you may be looking for someone who would be willing to do so in her place. So, I anticipated the possibility you now present to me."

The threesome again nodded, appearing to be relieved I had already considered this scenario.

"In fairness to you, though, I need to be up front about something I've begun to consider in the last few years. It has to do with our judicatory's pastoral remuneration system." A couple of frowns slowly displayed on the foreheads of the two men on the committee.

"How so, Bob?" asked Thornton.

"Well, ever since arriving in the area and becoming a member of our judicatory, it's annually intrigued me that the pastoral remuneration system is pretty broad. Each congregation is at liberty to offer salary packages that vary pretty substantially from one church to the next. For example, the smallest congregations this year are expected to pay a minimum of $28,500 to their pastor. That's what the two smallest actually are doing, according to their annual reports. But the largest congregations apparently are allowed to pay in excess of $60,000 to their pastor, according to their own reports."

Before I managed to continue, Thornton interrupted. With a patronizing smile he said, "Not sure what that has to do with our work here this afternoon, Bob."

"Well, Thornton, it has to do with the annual responsibility of the president to deliver his or her President's Report at the spring gathering. In that report the president is tasked with sharing his or her assessment of the judicatory's condition, and is invited to bring recommendations accordingly."

"We all know that, Bob," interrupted Thornton a second time. "Still not sure what the salary stuff has to do with your possibly serving as the next president."

"It has to do with what I've decided is a likely focus of my President's Report a year from this spring were I to be elected. I anticipate the real likelihood my Report would highlight the shocking disparity in pastors' salaries. I anticipate I may well recommend a judicatory-wide study of how to foster a more equitable salary system."

A third interruption: "Where's this all coming from?" queried Thornton, earlier smile now a thing of the past.

"It's coming from an increasing concern, even conviction, that budgetary disparities from congregation to congregation betray some pretty unhealthy financial ethics in our midst." I collected myself for a moment, while all three waited. I continued. "In the last couple of years I've had some fascinating and illuminating conversations. Some have been with the pastors of two of the smallest congregations in our judicatory. When I've pressed them, both have acknowledged their congregations can't afford to pay them more than the absolute minimum salaries allowed. But each of them has a family they're trying to support, and it's taking a significant toll on their marriages, their kids, and their own emotional sense of worth.

"I've also had some remarkable discussions with a dear friend who happens to be a Roman Catholic priest in a parish in the same village as my own congregation. When asked, he informed me that every priest in the entire diocese receives the same stipend, no matter the size of his parish. The priest in a parish with two hundred parishioners receives exactly what his counterpart in a parish with two thousand receives." I stopped, caught my breath, and noted looks of perplexity if not ire on the faces of the two male members of the nominating committee. The female member had the makings of a slight smile on hers. "I understand the rationale oftentimes used to explain the wide spectrum of salaries in our own judicatory: 'larger churches are more demanding of their pastoral leadership, their members expect their pastors to receive compensation comparable to that of their typical members,' and so forth. But I'm less and less convinced those reasons should hold sway. I'm more and more convinced we as the church are meant to model different standards—more biblical approaches—to pastoral remuneration. I truly believe we can learn from our Catholic friends."

Thornton started chuckling, looking over at his male friend on the nominating committee. "Well thank God we're not Catholic!" he chortled. The two men guffawed, while their female counterpart remained silent. As did I.

I continued. "So I thought it best to give you a little heads up. If I were to be elected as the next president of our judicatory, I anticipate urging the whole body to give strong consideration to doing serious study of how we model stewardly support of all our pastors. That would include intensive inquiry into how our larger congregations might be called to provide some support to our smaller congregations, enabling those congregations to offer more equitable remuneration to their pastors and their typically young families. That kind of help could result in those pastors staying in those churches longer than they currently seem to be doing."

With that, I stopped.

What can only be described as awkward silence ensued—not to my surprise, I should note.

"Okay then, Bob. I'm glad you shared all of that with the three of us," said Thornton. He looked at the other two. They nodded agreement.

Then the female member spoke for the first time since welcoming me a good bit earlier. "I really appreciate what you've been thinking about, Bob. Important issue." Upon which she was given looks of surprise, if not irritation, by her two male counterparts.

"Yeah, well, thanks for driving over, Bob," chimed in Thornton. "We'll be in touch, I'm sure."

Within a minute or two I exited his large study, walked to my car, and headed home.

I never heard back from the nominating committee. Not one word.

Do I know with certainty why? No. But I confess, even years later the reason seems too obvious to ignore, much less deny. It had to do with money. Or maybe more to the point, it had to do with power, with privilege, with influence. I'm not sure which word best applies, but I am sure even the threat of urging the twenty some churches' leaders to ask important questions about salaries and such was enough to torpedo any further consideration of my nomination.

Did I regret forewarning the threesome about the hypothetical possibility of bringing this issue of equity before the judicatory in the context of the annual President's Report? Again, no.

But some fifteen months later, I sat and listened to the report of the pastor who actually ended up being nominated and elected as president. His report glowingly lifted up the health of every congregation, celebrating how all the parishes were living examples of God's call to live in justice and compassion. Squirming in my seat, I found myself succumbing to the biblical practice of the gnashing of teeth. My own.

37

Enlightened

CLAIRE ASKED HER QUESTION with simple, unassuming curiosity. But as I let the question's implications sink in, I found myself speechless. "Pastor Bob," Claire had begun, "was that woman helping Jesus see for himself for the first time that he was supposed to be the Messiah of not just the Jews, but of *all* people?"

Along with a dozen other adults, Claire and I were engaged in a Sunday morning Bible study of the Gospel according to Matthew. For a number of weeks we had been working our way through that book, and had now come to the fifteenth chapter (verses 21–28), reading the following aloud:

> *Jesus left that place and went away to the district of Tyre and Sidon. Just then a Canaanite woman from that region came out and started shouting, "Have mercy on me, Lord, Son of David; my daughter is tormented by a demon." But he did not answer her at all. And his disciples came and urged him, saying, "Send her away, for she keeps shouting after us." He answered, "I was sent only to the lost sheep of Israel." But she came and knelt before him, saying, "Lord, help me." He answered, "It is not fair to take the children's food and throw it to the dogs." She said, "Yes, Lord, yet even the dogs eat the crumbs that fall from their masters' table." Then Jesus answered her, "Woman, great is your faith! Let it be done for you as you wish." And her daughter was healed instantly.*

For several minutes our circle of a dozen adults had then commented about the scene Matthew describes. One of the men in our circle noted the Canaanite woman shouting at Jesus would likely have caused him to echo the disciples' pleading with Jesus to send her away. "Nobody likes a loud mouth," griped the man, earning looks of disapproval from more than one of us in the circle.

One of the women in the circle then asked, "I wonder why Jesus chose to travel all the way to Tyre and Sidon, so far from his homeland?"

"Seems like maybe he was on a kind of sabbatical from his ministry," suggested another, prompting some smiles and nods of agreement.

But after a moment or two of quiet, another asked with understandable solemnity, "Was Jesus calling that Canaanite woman and her daughter *dogs*?"

Everyone in our group swiveled their heads in my direction. The question was clearly unsettling, given its implication—no, its unabashed indictment—that Jesus had a blatant distain for anyone who wasn't Jewish. Unable to dodge my parishioner's legitimate question, I responded, "There seems to be little question that's what he was doing." The look on everyone's face was one of surprise, if not discomfort. "It's pretty evident, given how Matthew recounts this incident, that in this moment Jesus was betraying a fairly typical, Jewish disregard for Gentiles—those who were not Jewish. It was the norm in his day for Jews to refer to Gentiles as dogs, which was the ultimate insult. Dogs were not pets, nor were they held in any affection in the Jewish culture."

"So what was Jesus saying then, Pastor Bob?" asked one of the women in the circle. "Was he saying to this woman, 'Your daughter doesn't deserve to be healed because she's a Gentile'?"

I sat there, feeling as unsettled as everyone else in the room. "Certainly seems so, doesn't it," I responded. "I'm not sure how else to interpret Jesus's saying to her, 'It's not fair to take the children's food—presumably what's intended for Jews, God's chosen people—and to throw it to dogs—presumably non-Jews, like that Canaanite woman and her demon-possessed daughter.'" Silence descended on the group.

That's when Claire, typically the quietest member in the circle, spoke up. "So, Pastor Bob, what Matthew's telling us is that Jesus went to a place where a non-Jewish woman approaches him and begs with a loud voice that he heal her daughter, and he at first refuses because she's not Jewish?" I nodded. "Jesus basically calls her and her sick daughter dogs who don't deserve the blessings God wants Jews to have?" I nodded again. Then, shaking her head in quiet wonder, she continued, "Kind of amazing to me what then happened." Looking down at the Bible in her lap, she said, "In spite of Jesus insulting both her and her sick daughter, she makes it clear that even dogs are allowed to eat food that humans let fall to the floor."

Now all of us in the group looked at Claire, back at our Bibles, and then at Claire again. She continued softly, "It's almost like that amazing woman was saying something Jesus *himself* had never thought about before." Silence around the circle. "It's almost like that woman was teaching Jesus something he had never considered before that very moment."

More silence, with all of us staring expectantly at Claire—a rarity, given her typically quiet demeanor.

"Pastor Bob, is it possible that non-Jewish woman was helping Jesus think about something he really *had* never thought about before?" Claire's question stunned me. And it stirred me. To the core.

"Say more, Claire," I responded quietly, gripped by the moment.

Claire sat there, looking down at the Bible in her lap. With not a sound coming from the rest of us, she asked, "Pastor Bob, was that woman helping Jesus see for himself for the first time in his life that he was supposed to be the Messiah of not just the Jews, but of *all* people?"

The discussion that ensued was holy. It was transformative. I confess it was the first time in my entire life I had ever given consideration to the possibility that Jesus, as fully human as divine, didn't have it all figured out from the first day of his three year public ministry. Until that moment of Claire's asking her bombshell question, I had unconsciously—yes, lazily—presumed Jesus always understood in full what his mission was to be. I had since childhood pictured Jesus as someone who always knew exactly what his purpose in life was. But now, in light of Claire's unimpeachable insight, I had to admit my previous picture of Jesus was overly simplistic. In fact, it was less than human.

What Claire helped all of us in that Bible study group begin to see was the unarguable fact that a Gentile woman, who had just been abominably shrugged off by Jesus as being a despicable dog, was the very one who may well have enabled that same Jesus to discover his own, fuller calling. It was she—and not any of the supposedly wise rabbis or scholarly priests at whose feet Jesus may have sat in his younger years—who may have helped Jesus see for the first time in his three decades of life that he had been sent by God to redeem not just Jews, but Gentiles, as well. And in this moment when she had done so, Jesus then immediately healed her daughter. It was as though Jesus came to realize in that very instant who he was, and to whom he had been sent as healer and redeemer.

Years later, as I recall that Bible study stunner coming in the form of Claire's honest inquiry, I remain profoundly indebted to Claire—and to the one who saw fit to bring her into the lives of the rest of us in that Bible study circle. Did Claire's insight derive from years of theological studies about Jesus? No. It came from her quiet but determined willingness to ask unsettling questions as an earnest disciple of that same Jesus.

Interestingly, the woman Matthew describes as shouting at the thirteen men from Israel has never been identified by name. The woman who was at first called—and treated like—a dog by those same thirteen men remains a nameless Canaanite, never to be heard from or written about again in Matthew's account of Jesus's life and ministry. But her legacy lives on, in no small measure, I believe, by the way in which Jesus himself may well have been changed by her. It was she, whom Jesus had at first grossly insulted, who may have helped Jesus discern—even discover—the boundless breadth of his messianic purpose on Earth.

Given the depth of respect I've had ever since for my dear parishioner in that Bible study circle, I've found myself drawn to name that Canaanite woman Claire, as well.

I thank God immeasurably for both women.

38

Missed

It didn't happen very often. But when it did, my heart would inevitably ache. It ached primarily for the person who felt they just weren't missed. It ached secondarily for the church family who had such a culpable role in that person feeling forgotten.

The above would come to light in the context of my week to week and month to month work of pastoral care. With the assistance of Rich, a quietly faithful member of the congregation, weekly worship attendance was tracked. On a frequently updated chart with the names of the congregation's members and adherents, Rich would make note of who was present in worship each and every Sunday. He would then leave that updated tracking sheet on my desk, enabling me each Monday morning to note who had been absent the day before. With relative frequency I would thus be able to spot an unexplained series of Sundays when one or another individual had not been in worship. I would then contact those individuals, oftentimes leading to the scheduling of a visit together.

More often than not those pastoral conversations with individuals who had been absent from worship would give me opportunity to hear how their lives were unfolding. Sometimes I would be regaled with accounts of joyful vacations out of town or of youth soccer leagues now scheduling games on Sunday mornings. Sometimes I would learn of a parishioner's exhausting trials in their workplace or school. And sometimes I would even be informed for the first time about abrasive tensions in a member's family or marriage. In those various instances, having noted the persons' absences, and then gently inquiring into their well-being, I was able to become better aware of their many life stories—including the strains that sometimes defined those stories.

More often than not, those follow-up pastoral conversations with individuals who had not been in worship for a few weeks proved beneficial. The parishioners would express their appreciation for having been missed. In due course, most of them would return to their earlier patterns of worship attendance, welcoming the blessing of being part of a congregational family who embraced their sisters and brothers, both in times of delight and in times of burden.

But on occasion those pastoral conversations with individuals who had been absent for a stretch would prove exceptionally painful. And I confess that though it didn't happen very often, when it did, the ache was deep.

On those occasions, for example, I might hear the hurting parishioner describe something akin to the following. "Pastor Bob, you may not know it, but for a while now there's been a drying up of my relationship with Reese Smith. Reese and I were friends going way back. My family and the Smiths picnicked together. Reese and I would cross paths at little league games. We'd work side by side at church events. It was good." Then the parishioner would tense up, with a look of both sorrow and anger. And they would say, "But Reese doesn't notice me anymore. Reese's kind of gone their own way, what with all our kids growing up and all. I've tried to reach out, but Reese pretty much ignores me—as if I don't matter anymore." And then: "So I stopped coming to church a while back. I guess I did it because of Reese. I missed Reese, but I wanted Reese to miss me, too." And that's when I would hear what caused my heart to break. "But since I stopped attending on Sundays, nobody's noticed. Not Reese. Not anybody. It's as though nobody cares. And if that's the case, why would I want to go back to church at all? I mean, I get it if Reese doesn't care that I'm not there. Our friendship is over, I guess. But I was hoping everyone else would care. I was kinda hoping others would see that I wasn't there, and would call me or something." Then, with tears streaming down their face: "But nobody noticed. Nobody called."

With that heart-rending declaration, a member of the church family reported to that family's pastor that they were forgotten. That they weren't even missed. And they likely would never again return to worship with their church family.

I share all of the above, not to cast blame, but to offer a reminder. We, the body of Christ, are given the gift—and opportunity—to embody the love, grace, and embrace of Christ. When we gather to worship—be it in a sanctuary or a living room, around a campfire or a gravestone—we are to do so as a family. We are to value everyone who is present. But we are also—and always—to do the same with those family members absent from our midst. Those out of view should matter to us as much as those in view. If not, those who are missing, for whatever reasons, may soon decide, maybe unbeknownst to anyone else, that they no longer matter. They may decide in their isolation they no longer belong, both to the church family, and even to the one who calls that church family into being in the first place.

Watch for those who are missing. They each matter. They each need to know, in the heart of their hearts, that they are missed. That they belong.

I sincerely believe there is no better news than knowing that one is missed. In fact, we might rightly call that *good* news.

39

Voice of the Victim

I WAS MID-STREAM DRAFTING the coming Sunday's sermon when she called. I answered the phone and heard Regina say, "Pastor Bob, I've written a letter and I want to show it to you before I mail it. Can I bring it by in the next few minutes?"

With no idea what she was referring to, I said, "Of course, Regina. I'm here in my study."

"I'll be right there." Click.

I sat at my desk, befuddled. And curious, I realized. Regina was a highly regarded member of my congregation. I had seen her, along with two of her friends, the previous evening at a fairly large celebration in the gathering hall of a nearby congregation. Well more than a hundred adults from area churches had come together in order to share in a send-off party for a pastor who was moving out of state to begin a new job. The adults in attendance had included pastors and laypersons who had had the privilege of benefiting from his ministry. Regina and her friends, along with several other members of my congregation, had been part of the evening's festivities.

It was now barely a dozen hours since Regina and I had waved goodbye at the close of the celebration. Into my study she walked, with a look on her face that betrayed a surprising mixture of sadness and fury. I stood up to welcome her, and before I even managed to say, "Good morning," she stuck her arm out in my direction, at the end of which was a sheet of paper. "I want you to read this. I'm not looking for your approval or disapproval. I just want you to know I'm putting it the mail this morning."

A bit of a chill ran down my spine on hearing her words and taking in her facial expression. "Of course, Regina." I took the sheet from her, still looking her in the eye. "Is there anything I should know before I read it?" I asked.

"You'll find it self-explanatory, Pastor Bob" She nodded at it, signaling her insistence I proceed to read. I sat down, as did she, with nothing more said between the two of us for the next few minutes.

It was a photocopy of a formally typed letter, including Regina's home address and last evening's date at the top. It was addressed to another pastor in the denominational assembly of which I was a part.

> *Rev. John Smith:*
>
> *This evening you crossed the line, both as a pastor and as a citizen. You and I had never met before this evening, though I knew of you by name. When I sat down with my two friends in order to enjoy some food and fellowship, you happened to be sitting at the same table, opposite us. Before I knew what was happening, you looked at me and said, in front of my friends, "My, I don't think we've met before." You proceeded to look at my body in a way that made my skin crawl. You ignored my friends, continued to stare at me, and said, "How come I don't know who you are?"*
>
> *Your doing so immobilized me. There was no reason for your speaking to me in that manner, much less asking me that ridiculous question, other than that you were coming on to me in a totally inappropriate manner.*
>
> *I tried to ignore you, both because I wanted to visit with my friends, and because I was feeling sexually objectified. I was astonished that the people sitting beside you, with whom you had been talking before my friends and I sat down at the same table, seemed to let you leer at me. In fact each of them looked away, as if they knew exactly what you were doing. That frightened me all the more.*
>
> *You persisted, asking me what my name was and which church I came from. When I said, "Regina, from Altamont Reformed," you smiled and said, "Ah, Regina." That was when I had had enough. I stood up and left the table, along with my two friends.*
>
> *I don't know who else observed your behavior, but I did. And upon arriving home, feeling both disrespected and assaulted, I decided to write you this letter.*
>
> *Your behavior towards me was wrong. I felt, and still feel, sexually objectified and harassed. That you engaged in that behavior in front of other adults, seemingly without restraint, is appalling to me. It suggests to me that what you did to me was not the exception, but quite possibly the rule.*

> *Stop this behavior. I'm not begging you to do so. I'm insisting on it, and will not hesitate to follow-up with more serious action if your behavior does not stop.*
>
> *Regina Jones*

When I finished re-reading the letter, I looked up. Regina was sitting absolutely still, her eyes red. But there were no tears any longer. Only an expression that betrayed a sleepless night. "Regina, I'm so, so sorry." She nodded. "I wasn't aware of what happened to you," I added.

"You weren't at the table, so you wouldn't have seen it." I nodded, about ready to respond. But before I said a word, Regina continued. "I wanted you to have a copy of this letter and to be aware that man will be getting it in a day or two. I have no idea what he'll do once he reads it, but I thought it fair to you to alert you ahead of time, in the unlikely case he calls you, since he now knows I'm a member of your congregation."

"I appreciate that, Regina. But I'm feeling really, really distressed on your behalf, not to mention furious about John." I stopped, and then said, "Would it make sense for you and me to share in this communication?"

Apparently anticipating that question, Regina stoutly declared, "No. It's my letter. It's for me to call him out, and it's for me to let him know I'll be watching from now on."

"Would it help you for him to know you've shared this letter with me?" I asked.

"I've thought about that. But no, Pastor Bob. This letter will stand on its own." Then, before I could respond, Regina stood. With undeniable determination. With unarguable fortitude. She departed, presumably for the post office.

For a long stretch I sat quietly at my desk, sorting through all Regina had shared with me. She had given me a photocopy of her letter, but by insisting the letter was from her—and her alone—she was asserting her own authority. Her own standing, including in the male-dominated world of the institutional church. Her voice was her voice. She needed no male voice to give it validation.

A number of days passed before Regina and I spoke again. I had called her and inquired how she was faring. She indicated she was doing fine. Mailing the letter had been transformative for her. When I asked if she had heard anything back from Rev. Smith, she sighed over the phone, saying, "Of course not. Men like him never respond to those who call them out. That would be both acceptance of responsibility, and indication of maturity."

We agreed to meet in person the following day. When we did, I realized how great my respect for Regina was, and would remain. She clearly still bore the wound of being objectified, of being harassed in ways men can never fully fathom. Yet she displayed a strength, a determination, that both humbled and inspired me.

Two months thereafter, while sitting in a quarterly gathering of our denominational assembly, it all came back to life. Out of the blue, during the portion of the agenda entitled New Business, Rev. Smith stood amongst the sixty of us in attendance. In a matter of fact manner, he posed a question to the presiding chairperson, and therefore to the entire assembly, comprised primarily of male clergy and elders. "Do we have any updated policy about sexual harassment in the church these days?" The chairperson, clearly unprepared for such an inquiry at that moment, shrugged. "Just interested," said Rev. Smith with a blank expression on his face. "I recommend the executive committee research it and get back to all of us." He then sat back down. The chairperson, still puzzled, shrugged again, and then nodded towards the recording clerk to make note of the recommendation. No discussion ensued.

Sitting on the far side of the large meeting space, I found myself staring at Rev. Smith. Even when other agenda issues were then raised and discussed, I couldn't stop staring, waiting for him to steal a glance in my direction. No such glance came my way. He sat in his seat, studying intently whatever papers he happened to have in his hands.

Six months later a draft of an updated policy about sexual harassment in the church was circulated for study. Three months thereafter that updated policy was affirmed. Unanimously.

I confess all too frequently over the years I have felt an irresolvable embarrassment—even culpability—about my share in the corrosive ways we male pastors have often assailed the vulnerable ones meant to be in our shepherding care. All too often, and in all too many ways, we make a mockery of our calling by the ways in which we subtly, sometimes brazenly, abuse those whom we are meant to serve.

Regina is one such victim of that abuse. But she was, and remains, someone far more to me. She represents a conviction of dignity, a voice worthy of respect, a person of inestimable value. She embodies—yes, embodies—whom it is our creator indwells and through whom our creator calls us to task. Calls us to repentance. Calls us to renewal.

I remain honored to call Regina my sister in Christ. I look to her, and to so many of her sisters, to show us the way to restoration.

40

Neighbor

I HAD JUST PARKED my car a little ways down the block. As I walked towards the front door of the church building five minutes before our pastors' support group was scheduled to convene, Martin caught up to me. The host pastor for that month's support group meeting, Martin had just stepped out of the parsonage next door. He welcomed me as we then walked in tandem towards his church's main entryway.

It was then that the look on my face—one of bemusement, if not confusion—did not escape Martin. He nodded, and then smirked, at the three foot wide, totally unkempt portion of lawn at which I was staring. It ran in a long, straight line between the church building and the private home on the side of the church opposite from the parsonage. On either side of that hundred foot long, frumpy line of unmown grass and weeds, the lawns of both the church and the neighbor were in beautiful shape. And because the two lawns were in such well-tended condition, that dividing line of wild, untended turf was all the more obvious. In fact, it almost shouted out to passersby, "These neighbors really don't care much for each other."

Seeing me stare for a moment or two at that long line of overgrown nature, Martin said, "That's the informal border between the Johnsons' land over there and the church's land over here. At least we all think so," he added. When my facial reaction signaled my inability to make much sense of his explanation, he continued, again with a smirk. "You see, Bob, for several years whenever Mr. and Mrs. Johnson's grandkids came to visit them, those kids regularly wandered onto our church property whenever they came out of the Johnsons' house to play." He stopped, as if his explanation was sufficient. Seeing my ongoing look of bewilderment, he continued. "Don't you see, Bob? Their grandchildren would play over here on the church's lawn, and sometimes they'd leave their toys here, and would even make messy snow angels and weird looking snowmen out of *our* snow during wintertime. When we'd ask the Johnsons to keep better tabs on their grandkids, Mr. Johnson would tell us the kids were only playing on their property, not the church's." Glancing over at the Johnsons' house next door, Martin said, "So we kinda got into an ongoing debate about where their property ends and the church's begins. We didn't ever come to a formal agreement." Then, pointing at that three foot wide, hundred foot long swath of tall weeds that ran from street to back yard fence, he said, "That line is what came from our disagreement." To my dismay, his declaration sounded like one of unabashed pride, and even of delight.

"So," I began slowly, "the Johnsons and you both decided not to mow that long line of grass and weeds between your properties?"

"That's right, Bob. We didn't discuss it or anything, but I let our church groundskeeper know not to mow there about the same time Mr. Johnson apparently decided the same thing." Then, swinging his arm toward that ugly demarcation line between church building and neighbor's house, he stated, "Now we all know where our properties begin and end. No more kiddie toys scattered around our lawn in the summer, and no more messy snow angels and crude looking snowmen in the winter, either."

With that, Martin headed into the church building. I followed, now both confused and irritated. Together with pastoral peers from half a dozen parishes, two hours of conversation then unfolded, but with little focus coming from me. I could not in the least make any sense of what Martin had just disclosed. I confess, in fact, that sharing in any supportive conversation with Martin during that time felt artificial, if not impossible.

Driving home to my own parish, I continued to mull over the picture of that odd borderline between church and neighbor. In doing so, the Korean peninsula, of all places, came to mind. Midway between the still warring north and south portions of that peninsula lies the DMZ—the demilitarized zone, where the Korean neighbors agreed back in 1953 to remove their military forces while remaining in an informal state of war. That historic metaphor made my skin crawl, given the introduction to Martin's ecclesiastical version of a DMZ having been begrudgingly, if not cruelly, created between church and next door neighbor.

But then something happened to me. Still driving homeward from Martin's church, a memory from the distant past seeped its healing way into my thoughts. The memory was of a very brief but incalculably impactful exchange I had had with my beloved older brother, Don.

I was almost twelve back then, and was getting my initial lesson in how to mow a lawn. The previous fall our family had moved into our own first-ever house in the U.S., having just uprooted from Lebanon. When the following springtime arrived, our father tasked Don with the weighty responsibility of teaching me how to mow our home's little lawn, using an old, used push mower from the 1950s. For the better part of an hour, I pushed that weighty gizmo up and down the front lawn, working from one side of the house that had a well kept hedge between our home and that of that neighbor, all the way to the other side, which had no such hedge boundary. By the time I reached that unbounded piece of lawn between our house and that of the second neighbor, I remember trying to gauge by naked eye where the boundary actually was. My adolescent brain told me to be sure to mow all the way up to that line, but no further. That's what I did. Our house's grass was tightly trimmed up to the line that was perfectly perpendicular from street side to back yard—a line clearly demarking the boundary exactly midway between our house and our neighbor's, but not a foot, or even an inch, beyond.

As I then stood there, sweating but proud of my efforts, Don walked up and said, "Nope. You can't stop where you've just stopped."

I looked at him, a bit perplexed. "What do you mean?"

"Bob," he said gently, "you should always mow at least one row beyond the boundary between your house and your neighbor's." When my look told him I was missing his profound point, he explained, "Good neighbors extend themselves." Again, my look of confusion. "We're supposed to be good neighbors. Good neighbors to the Smiths next door should make it clear we're here to help them with their work, including mowing the grass. When we mow one row onto their lawn, it's our way of saying, "We're happy you're our neighbors, and we're around to be of assistance whenever you may need it."

With that, Don patted me on the back, and gave me a little push, brother to brother, pointing at the unmown lawn right next to my already cut grass line. Taking his cue, I did as he advised. I mowed one more line beyond the artificial boundary between our two homes. And each and every time I mowed, all the way through my high school years, I did the same. And guess what: during that time our family's friendship with the Smiths grew and flourished.

Now, decades later, I drove into the church parking lot back in the parish I was serving as a fifty year old pastor. I parked the car, turned off the motor, and sat quietly for a time. It gave me opportunity to look around, seeing the various houses in proximity to the church building, both on our side of the street and across. Hearkening to the simple but transformative lesson my older brother had instilled within me some forty years earlier, I confess to tearing up. "These are all my congregation's neighbors. We are to be *their* neighbors," I whispered to myself. "Whatever boundaries may exist, whatever DMZs may have been silently assented to, whatever barriers may have been built up over the years between any of them and any of us—they do not belong."

And, of course, it wasn't just Don who so insisted. It was, and is, Jesus. (Matthew 22:39 and Luke 10:25–37)

41

Pastoring the Baton

WHAT JOLTED—ACTUALLY, ANGERED—ME WAS that the snarky comment was made by a fellow member of the clergy.

It was a Monday evening in mid-October. I was one of a dozen ministers who were on an overnight retreat at our denomination's beautiful camp in the Adirondacks. A few months earlier I had received an invitation to be part of this gathering composed of pastors who were fast approaching retirement. The preceding summer my wife and I had discerned that at the close of the following calendar year it would be time for the two of us to conclude our careers, she as a member of the faculty of a nearby medical school and I as the pastor of the treasured congregation I had served for three decades.

That autumn the overnight retreat with fellow clergy unfolded in very meaningful ways. Most of us knew one another at least moderately; some of us were very close friends. For me, that included Greg, a pastor of a congregation only ten miles from my own. It also included Jordan, an ordained clergyperson who was not the pastor of a congregation, but instead served as a specialized staff member in a local ministry to the homeless.

The respect Greg, Jordan, and I had for one another was high, given any number of occasions over the years when we had offered support to each other when one of us happened to be confronted with challenges, if not burdens, in our respective ministry settings. But while Greg and I were very soon approaching retirement, not so with Jordan, who was more than a decade our junior. Nonetheless, the retreat designers invited the younger Jordan to attend in order to be a small group facilitator for the rest of us older, soon to be retirees.

It was in his role as facilitator that younger Jordan's snarky comment prompted quite an explosion.

The clock read nine p.m., our agreed upon time to shut down our conversation and head to bed. For more than an hour our small group had been sitting in a circle of comfortable lounge chairs, aptly in front of the retreat center's blazing fireplace. The conversation had rambled a bit, following an early evening presentation by a special guest speaker. In due course, the discussion had veered in the direction of the anticipatory sadness all of us in the circle—with the exception of Jordan—were already experiencing as we envisioned saying farewell to our congregations. It also included one or two comments about how important it would be for each of us to prepare our respective congregations for the transition they would each have to make, adjusting from us, their retiring pastor, to our successor, their next pastor.

That was the moment Jordan said, "I have a strong suspicion about all of you." Since he hadn't spoken for several minutes, the others of us in the circle swiveled in his direction, totally ignorant of what he was intimating.

"A strong suspicion?" Greg asked Jordan.

"Yes," responded Jordan, with a little smile. Maybe even a smirk. "I suspect each of you actually hopes your successor flops. Big time."

For probably two or three seconds at most, the rest of us in the circle stared in silence at Jordan. But it was not a peaceful silence. *Au contraire.* Just as I was about to blurt out my reaction to Jordan's snarky statement, Greg beat me to it. "You suspect we want our successors to *flop*?" His face turned, almost instantaneously, a ferocious red. As did mine, I suspect. "How on earth could you *say* such a thing?"

Silently glancing back and forth between Jordan and Greg in the next few moments, I confess to feeling shocked. Even enraged. But before I managed to verbalize my own ire, Jordan responded. "Whoa, whoa, whoa." He actually put his hands up in front of his chest, involuntarily offering a gesture of self-protection. And with good reason: all four of us pastors, soon to be retiring, were glaring at him. "I was just joking!" He put his hands down slowly, and continued, "I just meant that maybe, when we retire, we don't want to be outshined by our successor, that's all."

That's when I found my voice. "Jordan, I can't tell you how much I want my successor to be a gifted, productive pastor. The congregation deserves it. They *need* it." I tried to control my voice from erupting. "I truly would never want anything but the *best* for my congregation when I retire." The others nodded in intense agreement.

"I get it. I get it," said Jordan in response. "I'm sorry. It was a stupid joke. Forgive me."

It took the better part of the next hour, well beyond our originally planned terminus, for the five of us to unpack the nature of Jordan's attempt at humor. What we had to acknowledge—with Jordan taking the lead, to his credit—was that his unsettling attempt at comedy betrayed what may well be a presumption, even if subconscious, amongst many in the wider institutional church. His suspicion about pastors possibly hoping our successors will prove less than capable, and even disastrously so, may be what some within the membership of our congregations also suspect. By that I most certainly do not mean that the congregations themselves want their new pastors to "flop." What congregation would ever want that to be the case? But if Jordan, a pastor himself, could even jokingly intimate that we *pastors* might hope for such a disaster, then might some members of our congregations not wonder just the same about us, their retiring pastors?

I sincerely hope the above is not the case. I earnestly desire that congregations have no reason to wonder about us, their retiring pastors, having any silent hope things will deteriorate once we pass the clerical baton to the next generation.

Now, years after retiring from the pastorate, I deeply yearn for the congregations I served to know I prayed fervently, and still do, that my successors would prove gifted in all they would contribute to the congregations' vitality and longevity. What pastor would—could—do anything but?

42

The Price Paid

SHOULD I HAVE BEEN as shocked—in truth, as enraged—as I was? Maybe not. Though the institution in question was an esteemed seminary, it was still an institution. It was still an institution constantly impacted by one of the influences under which essentially every institution suffers: money. Why should I imagine a seminary responding to that influence any differently than does any other institution in our marketplace economy? But I confess I had an implicit hope at least a renowned seminary might find it ethically and spiritually fitting to resist the influence of cold hard cash.

Now sitting at my desk, I realized how foolishly placed that hope was proving to be.

My shock—yes, rage—enveloped me as I re-read the lengthy email I had received just fifteen minutes earlier. The email was from a second year student enrolled in the seminary in question. I had met Emerson eighteen months earlier, just as he was preparing to graduate from college.

As an undergraduate senior, sensing a call into ordained ministry, Emerson had been accepted into the seminary's Master of Divinity program. Anticipating his theological education in that seminary, he also applied to be taken "under care" of a judicatory of congregations, including both his home congregation and the one I was serving as pastor. Being "under care" meant he was to be supported and examined during his seminary years by those of us in the judicatory's twenty congregations, with the goal of his being ordained after graduation.

So, some six or seven of us clergy and elders met as a committee with Emerson the summer after his college graduation, just weeks before he was to begin his studies at the seminary. We were immediately impressed with

Emerson. He was articulate, bright, engaging. He was forthright about his Christian conviction. And he was stirringly honest. He shared with us what he had chosen to share with everyone else in his world during the previous three years: he is gay.

During that lengthy "getting acquainted" conversation with Emerson, all of us on the committee explored with him what his being gay might mean for him in the coming three years on the seminary campus. When asked, he noted he had been fully forthcoming with the seminary throughout the application process. To our committee's relief, he stated he had received numerous assurances from seminary faculty and administrators that his being gay would not be problematic. He would be warmly welcomed on campus and would experience student life in ways fully comparable to that of all his fellow students who happen to be heterosexual.

Emerson subsequently traveled to the seminary and began his first year of course work. The year reportedly went well. Then, come springtime, he informed those of us on his support committee he had been accepted into a summer internship ministry working with inner city youth. He also noted, with some delight, the seminary's development office had approached him and requested he film himself during his summer internship. That office would then include his summer ministry's video account, with those of several other students, in a recruitment video to be placed on the seminary's website. The intent was to display the varied ways the seminary assists students in securing exciting ministry settings in which to engage in practical learning experience.

Summertime arrived. Emerson's work with the inner city youth unfolded, with one or two emailed reports from him indicating his thrill to be putting some of his book learning into practical ministry. He noted, as well, he was doing the requested filming for the seminary's development staff. I found myself looking forward to viewing his part in the promotional video once posted on the seminary's website sometime in the autumn months ahead.

But then came that moment when I found myself reading Emerson's email. When I found myself in shock. Enraged.

It was late September, several weeks after Emerson had completed his summer internship with the inner city youth and had returned to campus for his second academic year. His email in my shaking hands read, in part, as follows:

> Yesterday I was walking in the hallway, moving from one class to my next, when a staff person from the seminary's development office spoke briefly with me. He was walking from the opposite

> direction, spotted me, and called me by name. He proceeded to tell me the seminary had decided not to use my video in their recruitment video. When I asked him why, he said, "The president has told us there are a few members of the board of trustees who don't feel gays should be going into the ministry. He said we shouldn't expose you to any hard times. So, it would be safer for you if we didn't put you in the video."
>
> I told the director I was okay with them using my video, no matter what might come of it. I had come to this seminary, being fully open about being out. He responded by indicating the seminary president had made the decision for my own good, in order to protect me.
>
> I'm confused and pretty upset. I don't know what to do. So I thought it best to let you and the whole support committee know.

Having read and re-read Emerson's gut-wrenching message, I put the paper down and immediately turned to my computer. Trying to control myself, I typed an email to the other members of Emerson's support committee, describing to all of them what I had just learned. Within twenty-four hours several of us gathered for an emergency meeting.

It is not overstatement to report each and every one of us was beyond irate. The uniform consensus was that we should not only communicate our disappointment and support to Emerson, but that we should contemporaneously communicate our anger to the seminary president. Our ire was rooted in strong suspicion the president was being patronizingly dishonest with Emerson. We were convinced the president was hiding behind a veil of artificial concern to protect the student, when in fact he was frankly in fear of the seminary possibly losing out on a large sum of cash—in terror that one or more large donors, who may well be homophobic, would withhold future donations if and when they learned about the seminary's website highlighting a student who happens to be gay.

What especially galled all of us on Emerson's support committee was the apparent unwillingness of the president to come clean. To be truthful. While Emerson embodied transparent honesty, the president was opting for anything but. Under the guise of "protecting" Emerson—who from the day he applied for admission to the seminary, had been uncompromisingly and vulnerably honest—the president was choosing the less costly path of dishonesty. Emerson could see it, and so could all of us on his support committee.

Upon returning to my study at the close of the support committee's discussion, I drafted a letter over the signatures of the entire committee membership, addressed to the seminary's president. The essence of that letter was this: *You owe Emerson an apology. You owe him honesty, admitting your decision not to include his video was not motivated by some charitable concern for his protection, so much as for the financial welfare of the seminary. You owe him, and the wider church, a modeling of Christian institutional behavior empowered by fundamental integrity rather than financial angst.*

We mailed the letter.

We never received a response. Not one.

In retrospect several of us on the support committee came to the conclusion that receiving no response from the president did not mean our letter had no impact on him and his institution. Instead, the support committee came to presume the president may have been given specific counsel from the seminary's legal firm. That advice: *Don't respond. Any response could be interpreted as admission of culpability were a suit to be brought against the seminary. Safer to ignore the accusation than to respond in any way.*

Emerson, it should be noted, continued through his seminary education and has since entered into the ordained ministry. He reportedly received from the seminary no explanation, much less apology. Yet not surprisingly he maintained his dignity in the life of an institution that could have, and should have, learned from *his* very model.

And the seminary? I understand it received a sizeable donation from one of the trustees in the year or two after the Emerson filming debacle. Apparently the president's decision proved financially beneficial to the institution.

Years later it remains a question, in my mind and heart, what price was paid by the seminary. I wonder how much integrity the institution opted to forfeit for the sole purpose of receiving that donation at the expense of one of its most honest students.

43

Our Kin Joseph

EVER SINCE MY CHILDHOOD, the Old Testament figure known as Joseph has endured as a fascinating, even magnetic, character in my life. But in my sixty-eighth year my wonder about Joseph exploded to even greater heights.

My intrigue with Joseph began when I was five years old. I learned of this son of Jacob when white paper and colorful crayons were distributed in my Sunday school class. My teacher, Mrs. Thompson, invited all eight of us in the class to color the figure depicted in simple manner on that sheet. That figure? An adolescent boy, standing proudly out in the middle of a pasture of grazing sheep. He was wearing a bedazzling robe that just begged for colors. Mrs. Thompson explained that Joseph was the eleventh of twelve sons of a man named Jacob. She noted, in an understated way, Jacob decided to give Joseph the coat depicted on our sheets of paper—and that it was incredibly colorful. "Go ahead and color Joseph's coat," invited Mrs. Thompson. "Make it look as special as possible, because that's the way Joseph liked it!" Well, you'd have thought all eight of her Sunday school cherubs had just been welcomed into angel heaven. Each of us grabbed our crayons and had at it. Though my crayon box had only six colors, I managed to make dear Joseph's coat radiate with some dozen or more tones, mixing yellows and purples, reds and greens, and who knows what else. The result? A coat that Joseph's face suggested was the best thing since chilled goat's milk!

Almost twenty years later, sitting in a quiet cubicle in my seminary's library, I discovered Joseph anew. It was early in the first semester of my "Introduction to the Old Testament" course. I was tackling the incredibly detailed account of Joseph and his family as detailed in Genesis, chapters 35–50. I had never read straight through that entire collection of stories in serious detail. But in doing so now I found myself slack-jawed in astonishment at the wonderfully rich—and grievously unsettling—anecdotes comprising Joseph's life story. I knew of his father Jacob having given him "a long robe with sleeves" (Genesis 37:3b, whose traditional rendering in Greek translations is "a coat of many colors"). But I hadn't ever paid much attention to the unblemished—and inevitably family-destroying—fact that colorful garb suggested Jacob loved Joseph more than he loved any of Joseph's older brothers. And oh, by the way, the writer of Genesis notes, those siblings therefore "hated (Joseph), and could not speak peaceably to him." (Genesis 37:4b) That unvarnished fact embedded throughout the whole Joseph narrative gave me uncomfortable pause sitting in my cubicle. It evoked not only suggestive explanations of the gruesome events that followed in all of those brothers' lives. It *also* gave light to so much of humanity's fearsome, corrosive history over innumerable millennia.

The next night I returned to my library cubicle, continuing to wend my way through the gripping story of Joseph's life. I read of his vengeful brothers kidnapping him, stripping him of that perturbing coat their father had seen fit to bestow on him, and then selling him to passing slave traders. In due course those traders marketed him to Potiphar, an elite member of Pharaoh's court in Egypt. From there his story tells of his being sexually harassed by the wife of that elite. When Joseph resisted her advances, he was unjustly, albeit predictably, imprisoned. As most readers of Genesis well know, Joseph's astonishing story continued, ultimately seeing him released from prison because of a mysterious capacity to interpret dreams. When that interpretive gift was discovered and utilized by Pharaoh to the end of saving Egypt from the devastating effect of a forthcoming, seven-year long famine, Joseph ended up elevated to a position of unparalleled power, second only to Pharaoh himself.

Ultimately Joseph's story came full circle. As is so frequently taught in Sunday school classes and expounded in sermons from countless pulpits, Joseph was reunited with his brothers and father. Seeking relief from the famine devastating their home back in Canaan, Joseph's kin traveled south to Egypt. There, after much drama, Joseph revealed himself to his fratricidal siblings, and ultimately to their aging father—all of whom had long presumed Joseph never to be seen again. Their reunion was tear-filled. The restoration of brother to brothers was gripping. There are few if any more transfixing stories in all of the Old Testament.

But sitting pensively in my cubicle so many years ago, soaking in the enormous breadth of Joseph's life story, it was only then that a transfixing—and transforming—scene from his story began to overwhelm me. I confess I had never before noted it, much less felt its impact. It comes literally at the end of Genesis's lengthy account of Joseph—and actually of the lengthy book of Genesis itself. There in the final ten verses of Genesis's fifty long chapters, I read about his father Jacob's death, followed by an astonishing exchange between Joseph's older brothers and Joseph himself. Fearing Joseph would now exact revenge against his siblings for their hateful act of selling him to the slave traders decades earlier, those brothers begged his forgiveness. "But Joseph [then] said to them, 'Do not be afraid! Am I in the place of God? Even though you intended to do harm to me, God intended it for good, in order to preserve a numerous people, as he is doing today. So have no fear. . .'" (Genesis 50:19–21a)

Those last words quoting the aging Joseph bore their way into me. They managed to do so because, I realized, they disclose an astonishing perspective about God. Joseph was confessing to his older, fear-filled brothers that their God was, and is, creative in every sense of the word. Not only did their God bring all of creation, including humanity, into being. God continued—and continues—to work redemptively with that same creation. And with that same humanity. Joseph, after years of trying to make sense of the horrors of his family's fracture, had come to a remarkable discovery: God was not a passive observer of their family's travesty and tragedy. No. God was—and always is—at work to restore what is broken and to resurrect what is dying.

Joseph had come to recognize, and be humbled by, the wondrous reality that God takes what may be intended by humans for evil, and makes of it good. In the case of the older brothers' heinous plan to wipe Joseph out of their daily lives and their familial tensions, God then saw fit to take that plan and use it, irony of ironies, to save not only all of Egypt, but all of Canaan—including those murderous siblings themselves.

I confess tears trickled down my face while sitting pensively in the library. I was struck dumb with wonder at this image of God—as one who never scripts the horrors of human behavior, but again and again and again takes the travesties of humanity's story and from them births restored relationship.

"That's a God I could serve with gratitude," I said silently to myself, sitting in my library cubicle. And then: "*You're* a God I *will* serve with thanks, Lord," I found myself praying.

For the next four decades I was blessed with countless opportunities to share that good news. Repeatedly I discovered moments when I was invited to declare the astonishing truth our loving God never fails to take our human brokenness—even our violent, murderous propensities—and to fashion healing and renewal out of their ashes. Joseph's ageless story frequently found its way into those opportune moments.

Then it happened. More than five years after retiring from fulltime pastoral ministry, I was reintroduced to Joseph. And that reintroduction was breathtaking ...

Early into retirement my wife and I felt led to become members of a wonderful congregation that has a longstanding commitment of compassion for the forgotten and of embrace of the sidelined. Evidence of that commitment has come in many forms, one of which is intentional outreach to a nearby college's student body. That student body includes a small but significant number of those who self-identify as LGBTQ+.

The congregation has seen fit to create a variety of ministries in support of those all too easily isolated students, including the scheduling of a weekly gathering time to which any and all students are invited. That gathering time, planned and staffed by one of our congregation's pastors, unfolds in the basement of a house on campus designated for use by a number of minority groups who otherwise might not have a place to assemble for mutual support. On the same day each week in that basement our congregation hosts a gathering of those who are part of, or are supportive of, the LGBTQ+ community on campus. For ninety minutes students gather in the basement. They enjoy pizza, share in a Bible study, and end with Communion together.

It was to one of those basement gatherings that I was invited by the host pastor. She needed a clergyperson to fill in for her while she was on vacation. She explained that a student intern would take care of the food and would lead the Bible study. I could assist, she said, simply by overseeing the closing Communion time. I gladly accepted her thoughtful invitation.

I arrived on campus on the assigned evening. The student intern met me at the door and escorted me down the stairs into the gathering space. While she laid out the pizza and dishware, I prepared the Communion elements. Within minutes undergraduates began to arrive, clomping down the rickety stairwell to the basement. All present that evening were women, a dozen in number. They each briefly introduced themselves to me and then circled up around the large table. There we all sat, enjoying pizza and chatter. When the meal was over, the intern invited everyone to introduce themselves in full to everyone else, including sharing one's gender identity. I indicated I was cisgender male. The women disclosed a variety of orientations, including lesbian, bisexual, transgender, and non-binary. After all had greeted one another with a palpable warmth and acceptance, the intern announced it was time for our Bible study.

The intern grabbed her laptop, opened it on the large table around which we were still sitting, and said, "I've decided to read a sermon I found this past week. It's written by an Orthodox Jewish rabbi. She happens to be a lesbian." While the women around the table all nodded as if they had just been informed the sun would once again rise the next morning, I sat there in mild shock. I had no idea women were permitted to be rabbis within the Orthodox (read: very conservative) Jewish tradition. The fact that female rabbi was openly gay was an added surprise to me.

As I sat there doing my internal, rabbinic gymnastics, the intern proceeded, with all eyes on her. She read what proved to be a remarkable sermon preached by the rabbi about, of all people, Joseph. The same Joseph whose story had so impacted my faith way back in seminary, as well as ever since. The rabbi admitted to her fascination with who Joseph really was, given the weighty storyline of his life, from father-favored youngster to aging vice-regent in Egypt. Then, as the intern read from the screen of her laptop in a surprisingly matter-of-fact manner, the rabbi noted she is now increasingly convinced that Joseph was gay.

As soon as those simple words were read, I recall all dozen women around the table nodding in agreement. As they did so, the intern continued reading. "That he was gay is, of course, not something we can today prove beyond a doubt. But evidence suggests so. Though his thrill over his multi-hued coat may whisper as much, it's his older brothers' antipathy towards him that cries aloud that they suspected Joseph to be gay. Given the likely religious biases of the time, it stands to reason they therefore saw fit to evict him wholesale from the tribe." A little further in the sermon, the intern read the following. "That Joseph may have been gay would also lend credence to the chaos that ensued when Potiphar's wife tried desperately to seduce the handsome young man from among all of her husband's countless slaves. Joseph's rejection of her advances was both born of fear of Potiphar, and natural due to his orientation."

The intern read for the better part of ten to fifteen minutes. When she finished, the floor was open for discussion. What ensued was transformative for me. To a woman around that table, everyone noted concurrence with the rabbi's conjecture about Joseph, as well as delight that God saw fit to work through *him* throughout his hard life.

By the time our circle conversation wound to an end and we readied ourselves for the sacrament, I realized I, too, was in concurrence. The rabbi's simple but astute argument made sense. And, I realized, it broadened not just my image of who Joseph was. It deepened my wonder about our astonishingly gracious God.

In the next day or two I had a choice. I could do as so often I have done over the years: I could wax theological, examining the remarkable implications rooted in the Jewish rabbi's astute observations about Joseph and his God. By doing so I could then put pen to paper in an effort to prepare a case for discussion in the wider community regarding sexuality and the church.

But ultimately I chose otherwise. I opted instead to let my experience with those dozen women, all nodding in quiet agreement with the rabbi's reflections, to soak its healing way into my soul. And I allowed myself to welcome the gift of kinship with Joseph, just as his brothers ultimately did, and just as God invites everyone to do.

More than four decades after first being moved by the story of Joseph and God's redemptive work of saving countless lives in Egypt and Canaan through that same Joseph, I now find myself even *more* moved. The gift of being invited into that circle of amazing women in the basement, and of being allowed to share in their corporate celebration of God's use of that boy who loved his coat of many colors—such a gift is priceless. It continues to shape and *re*shape my faith, even as I soon enter the eighth decade of my life.

44

Unspeakable

It was 6:01 a.m. this morning, Good Friday of my sixty-eighth year on Earth. I awakened just enough to roll over in bed, hoping for another hour of sleep before rising for the day. That's when the pain hit. My left leg's long calf muscle, for whatever inexplicable reason, cramped.

If memory serves, it's been months, if not years, since I've experienced a calf cramp of such extreme intensity. For any and all who have had similar muscle cramps, it's likely that pain is all too familiar. The pain was sharp and immediate, and my unconscious reaction was to moan, if not groan. From comparable past episodes I remembered quickly my need to flex my toes upward, allowing the muscle to relax. With that goal in mind, I managed to shove the covers off my lower torso, sit up in bed, and force my aching leg to allow my toes to do their flexing thing. Gratefully, some ten to fifteen seconds into the episode my toes cooperated, my calf muscle relaxed, and the pain eased up significantly. For the better part of a minute I opted not to move, for fear of triggering another cramping assault. None came, prompting me carefully, oh so carefully, to lie back down, head on pillow, limbs as relaxed as possible.

The pain had essentially disappeared. But the anxiety about its possible return? It waned far more slowly.

There I lay, from 6:02 until sometime after 7:00. That hour was quiet. But my mind—and my soul? Not quiet in the least.

I lay there, staring at the ceiling, pondering that oh so brief—but oh so distressing—pain. And as I did so, I revisited the moving Maundy Thursday service my wife and I had attended not even a dozen hours earlier in our home church. I replayed the scenes depicted in the various Gospel passages read aloud during the worship hour: Jesus sharing in the sobering Passover meal with his disciples, initiating what we now call the Lord's Supper; Jesus agonizingly praying a few hours later in Gethsemane, asking that what lay in store for him might be taken away, but only if that be the divine one's will; Jesus being betrayed, abandoned, and denied by his own; Jesus being unjustly tried and brutally scourged, and then made to carry his own cross to Golgotha; Jesus being stripped and then nailed to that cross; and Jesus then hanging in agony on that cross for at least three excruciating hours, until he "breathed his last."

I lay there, staring at the ceiling, feeling a kind of spiritual embarrassment. The pain I had just experienced had lasted barely fifteen seconds. It had resolved almost instantaneously. But the pain Jesus had endured two millennia ago? The contrast caused me to lie there, mute and humbled.

And as I lay there, a memory flooded back from thirty-five years earlier.

* * *

It was mid-February of 1987. Ash Wednesday was fast approaching, and with it the season of Lent, culminating in the week the church has come rightly to call holy. I had for several weeks begun to do the requisite outlining of sermon possibilities for this meaning-filled season of the church year. That's when I found the magazine in my church mailbox on a Monday morning.

Nathan, a member of the congregation, had left for me the February issue of a scientific journal to which he subscribed. On the cover I found a post-it note. It read, "Pastor Bob, I think you'll find the article that starts on page 18 of serious interest." I took the journal into my study. After sorting through my weekly to-do list, I began to read the article and found myself transfixed.

The article was authored by two physiologists—experts in the field of living organisms and their parts. Their focus in this piece? Crucifixion, as horrifically designed by the Persian and Roman empires, among others, going all the way back to the sixth century BCE. The authors, who self-identified in their article as Christian, described over several lengthy pages the bitterly cruel dynamics of being crucified. They detailed how the perpetrators of this heinous act melded together two basic elements in order to maximize the pain and agony of the victims. They noted that victims were impaled in such a way as to cause them to die, not by bleeding to death, but by suffocating to death. Hanging on the cross, the physiologists noted, caused victims to sag so low as to put weighty pressure on the diaphragm, thereby impeding their ability to take a full breath. Victims had to pull down on their wrists and push up on their feet in order not to suffocate. But the nails impaling the wrists and feet were localized in such a way as to cause unspeakable pain in doing so. The net result, according to the physiologists: the crucified persons, desperate to breathe, caused themselves additional pain by pulling down on their wrists and pushing up on their feet. And ultimately, most cruelly of all, the victims were the ones who made the decision when to die. Be it from utter exhaustion or excruciating pain, at the last they chose to end their own life by ending the pulling and pushing—all while being observed passively and masochistically by those who had nailed them to the crosses in the first place.

I read the article through in its entirety. I sat at my desk, both nauseated and enraged. Not at the authors, nor at Nathan for having seen fit to leave it for me in my mailbox. I was nauseated by the sheer demonic nature of this human travesty, and enraged by the image of countless victims of the travesty over too many centuries.

Then, of course as Nathan intended, I found myself thinking of Jesus on the cross. Of his hanging between two other comparable victims of this monstrous act. Of his writhing in pain, his wrists and ankles in unending distress. Of his pulling and pushing up, trying to get his next breath before asphyxiation overtook him. And of his speaking through it all, at least in seven instances during those interminably cruel three hours before he chose the moment of his last breath.

Sitting immobile at my desk, it was those seven instances—what the church has come to call his last words—that then drew my quiet consideration. It hit me I had never, ever read those words in a physiologically accurate manner. I had never read them, be it silently to myself or aloud to a gathered congregation in the sanctuary, in a manner even mildly similar to their historical essence. To the contrary, for example, when I had read Luke 23:34, I had always read Jesus's words—"Father, forgive them; for they do not know what they are doing"—without stopping. I had always read that astonishing prayer as if Jesus had been able to intone it without catching his breath. But he could never have done so—not while crucified, desperate for each and every breath. Far more likely, Jesus would have been heard to gasp out, "Father." Then, pull and push, breathe in and only then breathe out, saying with a painful gush of air, "forgive." Then again, pull and push, breathe in and only then breathe out, saying, "them." The whole prayer, gasped out in Aramaic or Hebrew—twelve words in English—likely lasted the better part of a minute of exhausting effort, given the demands already being made on the one offering that prayer for those looking up at him from the foot of his cross.

I sat with the journal article on my desk for the better part of that Monday morning. I confess I was unsure what to do with it. The following morning arrived, and I headed off for the weekly meeting with my village's dear Lutheran and Catholic pastoral counterparts. Still unsettled by what the article had stirred within me over the previous twenty-four hours, I shared with Keen and Bob the essence of the authors' description of crucifixion. When I finally stopped talking, to my shock Keen said, "Well, that's what you need to preach about at our village's ecumenical Good Friday service in early April."

I looked at him in disbelief. "You think I should share in gruesome detail from the pulpit what the article discloses about what Jesus truly went through on the cross?"

"No," he responded. "You shouldn't do it from the pulpit. You should do it from out in the middle of the chancel, with nothing between you and the congregation. And you should do it without a robe, so everyone can see clearly your arms, your torso, and your legs." I stared at Keen, slack-jawed. "This is enormously important, Bob. And I sincerely believe it's for you to do—for yourself and for all of us." Father Bob, the Catholic priest, nodded in solemn agreement.

Some two months later I stood before the ecumenical collection of nearly a hundred and fifty worshippers, ages five to ninety-five. I did as Keen and Bob had urged me to do. I described as the physiologists did what it was like for Jesus as he hung on the cross, laboring in tortured pain to keep breathing, one breath at a time. I was anxious beyond measure that one or more in attendance might inform me after the service that this disclosure of the harshest realities of Jesus's crucifixion was too much for them. But not one did. To the contrary, the uniform response seemed unarguably to be one of undiluted awe at Jesus's sacrificial love. Of humbled wonder at Jesus's willingness to endure unspeakable pain on behalf of a world in desperate need of redemption.

*　*　*

Thirty-five years later, lying quietly in my bed this Good Friday morning, I allowed myself to picture Jesus, along with a thief on each side, struggling to breathe—agonizingly in pain, every time he did what his tormented body demanded in order to survive one more minute. As I did so, I teared up at the sight and the sound. I confess I wept, knowing what an insignificant moment I had just endured with a fifteen second muscle cramp that had me moaning, if not groaning. I wept, allowing myself to envision Jesus enduring infinitely more pain, experiencing unspeakable agony, and yet still speaking.

I heard him gasp words of forgiveness for his murderers, and of salvation to a thief who had only asked to be remembered. I heard him gasp words of familial hope to his mother and disciple, and of desperate thirst to any who might have compassion in the moment. I heard him gasp words of his fear of being forsaken by his God, and of resolved conviction that his life—and his life's work—were complete. And I heard him gasp words that his spirit was no longer in his own hands, but solely in those of his heavenly abba.

I am—we are—the recipients of the blessings embedded in those words. Of the love that brought them to Jesus's very lips in those cruelest of hours.

45

Old Friends

Before I realized it, it had begun to happen. I didn't start humming aloud, per se. But the tune—along with the timeless, moving lyrics—worked its way to the fore. Into my soul. From almost fifty years earlier, "Old Friends" seeped into the present and stirred the emotions of this almost sacred moment.

Phil and I were sitting beside each other on a simple bench. Together, we had claimed a relatively quiet corner of a small park a two-minute walk from the senior living facility where Phil's little apartment would prove to be his final dwelling place.

Born in the Netherlands, Phil had emigrated with his parents to the U.S. after surviving his teen years during the horrors of Nazi occupation. Ultimately, he became an esteemed professor of psychology on the faculty of the college I attended in Michigan, where I had known of him by name and reputation. But our personal friendship wasn't born for another half century, when he was in his early nineties and I in my late sixties. Both now retired, we shared membership in a small but dynamic group of aging gentlemen in the congregation of which we both were members. Over the course of a few years, Phil and I became better acquainted and agreed to meet for informal conversation. More often than not, those visits were in that small park near his senior living facility. The topics covered from visit to visit ran the gamut. Often they included mandatory updates on how the Dutch national soccer team was faring in international competition. Sometimes they focused on the vagaries of politics, or the wonders of the human mind. Always the conversation was refreshing and restorative.

But on this particular occasion, our conversation in the park was pronouncedly weighty. It was in fact about dying. For a recent stretch of time Phil had been undergoing medical care for prostate cancer. On his request I had served as chauffeur to and from his regular visits with his oncologist, sitting beside him in the examining room and ensuring he was able to hear and retain the various pronouncements and directives from his doctor. Two days earlier his physician had indicated there were no more medical interventions available. Phil's life was drawing to an end. "It's likely a matter of only a few months, if not less, Phil," his attending had said quietly. Phil had nodded his understanding.

A few days thereafter, sitting on the bench in the little park, the two of us now reflected on life. Not on death, but life, even while dying. To my wonderment, Phil smiled as much as he teared up, talking almost poetically about his family, his colleagues, his friends. Words still prove inadequate in attempting to capture the recollections and sentiments exchanged.

That's when "Old Friends" began silently to come to mind. Though I didn't hum it aloud, the tune and its lyrics nonetheless welled up within me. Within my very soul.

A little background is in order.

Ever since its composition in the late 1960s "Old Friends" has been a hauntingly beautiful tribute to the gift of friendship in one's elderly years. Written by Paul Simon, who recorded the number with his then musical partner Art Garfunkel, "Old Friends" captures in word and melody some of the incomparable nature of human companionship, especially in old age. Its gripping lyrics include the following: *Old friends sat on their park bench like bookends . . . Winter companions . . . waiting for the sunset . . . Can you imagine us years from today sharing a park bench quietly? . . . . Time it was, and what a time it was, it was a time of innocence, a time of confidences.*

I was introduced to Simon's piece during my college years, when frequently I would listen to Simon and Garfunkel's wondrous album entitled "Bookends." The third piece on that album was the more renowned number entitled "America." But three pieces thereafter? "Old Friends." And it was inevitably "Old Friends" that repeatedly would prompt tears to flow down my cheeks. Back then, still only twenty-one, I somehow already sensed the incomparable blessing of having—and being—old friends. In fact, so resonant was that conviction, I still recall with absolute clarity what I insisted unfold in my parents' living room during Easter vacation of my senior year. That Sunday evening, back home in New Jersey, I asked Mom and Dad to listen with me to "Old Friends" played on their old Magnavox stereo. They allowed me my tears in doing so, and found themselves shedding some along with me—with warm hugs and even warmer smiles.

Now, nearly a half century later, I sat with my new "old friend" Phil. On a park bench. Waiting for the sunset. And though I did not hum it aloud, I knew—oh how I knew—what a "time it was . . . of innocence . . . of confidences."

Phil passed away less than two months later. My sense of loss on hearing of his death was profound. Again, there were tears. But those tears were not solely of loss. They were of gratitude. For the gift of being old friends, even if our friendship was born only in the last few years of his life.

Now, a handful of years later, I confess I am increasingly appreciative of the gift of old friends. Almost daily I find myself recalling individuals who have left their healing mark on my life. I think it fair to say those individuals number not in the dozens, but in the hundreds. Some go back more than sixty years, while others just sixty months. But each has been, and remains, a priceless gift. By way of examples . . .

There was Lenny, my best bud in junior high and high school. Lenny was a genius, not unlike his parents. His father was Emeritus Professor in the Mathematics Department at New York University, having earlier been a fellow graduate student and close friend of Nobel laureate John Nash, whose life story was told in the captivating film entitled *A Beautiful Mind*. Lenny tried to teach me how to think ten moves ahead while playing chess, and how to calculate the odds of winning in five-card stud. Not once did I defeat Lenny in chess, nor win many plastic poker chips while sprawled on his bedroom floor. But he never crowed about his victories. Instead, he repeatedly would ask with a grin, "Wanna play again?"

There was Glenn, my closest classmate in college. Soon to become an esteemed pastor in the United Methodist Church, Glenn challenged me to ask hard questions in our religion and philosophy classes, and was a ferocious competitor on the pick-up basketball court. And most significantly he insisted, tirelessly, I should get better acquainted with the roommate of the young woman he would marry the summer after college. That roommate's name was Mary, whom I would wed two years after Glenn and Nancy exchanged their marriage vows.

There was Gary, ten years my senior. An educator and missionary, Gary proved to be a quiet, faithful support and encourager during a year of relative isolation I experienced while serving as a volunteer with a Church mission station in Bahrain the year between college and seminary. He tutored me in how to order my daily lunch fare in a tiny Pakistani restaurant where the wait staff spoke no English and I knew not more than six words in Urdu. Weekly after worship he would track me down, look me in the eye, and ask if I had managed to make it through another week. He was instrumental in my being able to say, "Yes, thanks." Decades later I wish I had thought to add, "in no small measure because of you, Gary."

There was Henry, a quiet, studious undergraduate in Ann Arbor and a member of the wonderful parish I served as a pastoral intern between my second and final years of theological training. Henry faithfully attended every Friday evening "student pizza supper" at the church, shyly but persistently engaging in the subsequent Bible study conversations. When he came out to me, one on one in my little study at the church, that he was gay, he began to teach me what unblemished honesty and incomparable vulnerability are all about.

There was Thelma, a long-retired school teacher in the first parish I served as pastor. Thelma was stoop shouldered and diminutive in stature—barely four feet eight inches tall—but embodied quiet strength on a daily basis. It was she who regularly confronted others on the church's governing board to keep in mind "what Jesus would have to say" about whatever issue lay before us each and every time we convened. So much like the late Ruth Bader Ginsburg, Thelma quietly filled the shoes of a wise prophet.

There was Joel, a renowned veterinarian in my second and final parish. Joel embodied quiet thoughtfulness, but never hesitated to speak truth gently when it needed expression. On countless occasions, Joel offered a patient ear, and then insightful counsel. On more than one instance he quietly, privately welcomed my accounts of confusion, and even frustration, about the vocation I was trying to fill as pastor. Though an expert in canine cardiology, he knew as much about the human heart as that of his beloved furry patients.

There was Sallie, as faithful a member of my parish as any. Though early in her retirement, she doggedly displayed for all to see what it means to be a steady presence in everyone's life, be they kin or neighbor. Sallie lovingly helped to raise her daughter's son, providing patient attention to the management of his Type 1 diabetes. In the life of the church, Sallie readily stepped forward to help in any and all circumstances. In addition to regular attendance at virtually every worship gathering and adult education setting, she was the first to grab a rake or a broom or a folding table, and then to model what it means to serve.

There was Rich, an engineer by training and an educator to the core. A science teacher in the local middle and high schools for his entire career, Rich exemplified curiosity, coaching his innumerable students in the art of inquiry and discovery. As a result, he was regularly referred to as "my favorite teacher" by countless youth, including my own offspring. And in the life of the congregation, Rich quietly and steadily gave of himself in servant leadership, in music ministry, and even on the church softball team, proving himself the only teammate able speedily to beat out infield single after infield single.

There was Ellen, who with her dear husband Dick modeled a commitment to spiritual inquisitiveness that drew so, so many of us into both inner examination and enfleshed compassion. Again and again, I would find my way to Ellen and Dick's front porch, overlooking the village where we all lived. There she would invite one to ponder the imponderables, never feeling compelled to uncover answers but resolved to welcome the mystery of a God who loves us come what may.

There was Allen, a pastoral peer. For close to three decades, on a weekly basis during our gathering with fellow clergy, he would share in the parsing out of both the jolts and the joys of ministry. Capable of rafter-raising laughter, Allen was equally ready to underscore the need for quieting self-examination. His parishioners resonated deeply with that breadth of pastoral instinct, as did I.

There was Sister Mary Lou, a beloved peer in ministry for many, many years. Though restricted by the institutional church from engaging in certain sacramental roles because of her gender, Mary Lou nonetheless earned a place of uncompromised affection in the hearts of her Catholic parishioners—and for good reason. She embraced everyone with a mix of gentle grace and uncompromising justice. In Mary Lou's company and care, those easily overlooked by others were put front and center in her pastoral attention.

There was Diane, church organist extraordinaire. For close to three decades, Diane provided uncompromising commitment not only to the highest quality in music ministry, but to empathic support of everyone who volunteered to share in that ministry. Her choirs excelled in their contribution to worship services year-round. Each of the members of those choirs knew they mattered, in every sense of the word. And maybe most importantly, the tall, skinny pastor with whom Diane served all those years knew she would never hesitate to nix an unsingable hymn I may have suggested for a forthcoming Sunday. In doing so, she salvaged from ignominy countless worship services. I remain eternally grateful, as do all of our fellow congregants, for all she has done and all she has been.

And finally, there was—and always remains—Mary, my wife of close to half a century. It wasn't until the summer following our shared undergraduate commencement exercises that we fell in love. By then Mary was committed to begin medical school that fall in Michigan, and I was headed overseas for a year of volunteer mission service—and thereafter off to seminary in Connecticut. Anticipating the potential logistical challenges our educations, not to mention our subsequent vocations, would present to us were we ultimately to wed, I recall posing to Mary the question, "How are we going to make this work in the years ahead?" To which she said, simply but profoundly, "We'll make it work." She smiled while doing so. She was right. By God's grace, our life together has been full to the brim with opportunity to serve in medicine and ministry, and rarely if ever have we been impeded in doing so. To the contrary, we've been blessed with the humbling gifts of a shared life of creative challenge and satisfying service, as well as three offspring who continue to bring us joy and pride beyond measure. I could not have asked for a better partner in life.

So, I confess there are few if any more priceless gifts from above than friends. Especially old friends. They are evidence—even, dare I say it, proof—of God's inestimable love. Forever.

Printed in the USA
CPSIA information can be obtained
at www.ICGtesting.com
LVHW020825280424
778596LV00003B/10